GET CLEAN

BY
MARTIN JOHN
WITH OLIVER PRITCHARD

CONTENTS

INTRODUCTION

Cocaine completely and utterly destroyed my life over 30 years. I was a self-made millionaire from the slums of East London who came from nothing. By the age of 27 I had dozens of furniture shops, drove a Ferrari, wore a Rolex, had a stunning girlfriend with a pair of fake tits, and a jet-set lifestyle. Cocaine didn't give a fuck about any of that.

It snatched it all away and left me with nothing. It made me lose my business, which I'd built up despite coming from a very poor background with no formal schooling. It's had a terrible effect on my family. When I went off the rails I disconnected from nearly all of them. When I was a very wealthy young man they used to look up to me, but when I got heavily involved with 'the powder' that soon wore off and they steered well clear.

Cocaine took my personality away and destroyed who I was. It brought me nothing but misery. I lost myself. I lost my self-pride and my direction in life. It kidnapped me, and gave me a false identity. Cocaine took away my feelings. I've got three kids and I didn't spend a lot of time with them growing up. I rarely went to sports days or school fetes. On the odd occasion I did, I'd run to the toilets and do a bit of 'gear'. All my marriages went out of the window through my addiction. There was always money readily available, so maybe that softened the blow. But I was living in a bubble. Eventually cocaine stole my entire identity, which I didn't think could happen because I was a very strong person, albeit from a very rough background. I always used that as my 'joker in the pack' to get me through. But it wasn't enough to beat cocaine. The drug came along and captured me. I didn't expect that to happen, so I never planned for it. It captured me, and very nearly won. After 30 years on the gear I finally pulled through, but there's still a lot of long-term damage. I've got children who don't want to associate with me, full stop. I had a frayed connection with my family for many years. Cocaine stole precious time from the addict that is not replaceable. You don't see your children growing up, because half the time you're off your nut. The other half you're trying to get some sleep, or chasing the pound note to pay your drug bill or buy more gear. The addiction ripped me from limb to limb and I became a cocaine-filled monster, constantly buzzing off my tits.

As a young man, I always regarded myself as a switched-on fellow, determined to pull myself out of poverty. I did it, but it was stolen back from me by the dreaded white powder. Growing up, I always knew I'd have a problem with women. I expected I'd have rocky relationships, because that's the character I've always been. But I didn't see cocaine creeping up and grabbing hold of me for 30 years. It's like an illness. I didn't feel any emotions, because it took control. When you're a coke-head you're not in the driving seat, you're the passenger.

People who say they've got it under control are talking bollocks. I've met them. I've sat with them, slept with them, got drunk with them. I've sniffed cocaine with them. It takes over your life, and all you're concerned about is calling your dealer to get a bit of gear.

The most dangerous thing about cocaine is that it's such a likeable drug. Anyone who has a line of coke changes. They go from a van driver to the King of England in five minutes flat. They think they become this big powerful person and they get this big rush, a massive boost of confidence. You think it makes you better, but in reality it's the opposite. Your decisions and what comes out of your mouth are complete and utter rubbish. Every day is a struggle because you need to function. People say to me "You can't function on cocaine." You can. You can get up, or you might still be up, and have a wash, but you're always chasing another line. Cocaine will ruin anyone's life. Anyone who says it doesn't is talking bollocks. And anyone who thinks it's a cool thing to do, take my advice, it's going to end in tragedy.

At the height of my addiction I was sniffing more than £3,000 of coke a week. I'd regularly sit up with my ex-wife Karen and get through £1,500-worth of coke in a night. Before I got wealthy with the shops, which didn't take too long, I was using hundreds of pounds-worth of the stuff most weeks. When things started to kick off with the business I was dishing out thousands of pounds a week on the stuff. That's more than £12,000 a month up my nose. At my worst, I was using from the minute I got up until the early hours of the next morning. The next day I'd wake up feeling like shit and bang, I'd have two grams of coke to get me going after I'd necked a large vodka and lemonade. I'd do one nostril, one gram. It would give me this massive rush of energy and when I came down from it I felt fucking dreadful.

But I still kept on taking it. It got to a point that at one stage, after a five-day bender, I was taking so much coke I couldn't get any more up my nose. I went to sniff a line and it just fell out. I ended up eating it off a spoon, which was a dreadful experience.

Taking that much coke makes you disorientated. It makes you paranoid as fuck. Unfortunately, the people I was with at the time were all using coke, so we were all in the same boat. As I gradually lost my wealth and things got really bad, I'd spend a lot of time on my own, 'doing the gear'. That was the worst point of my life. Most people have company, or they sit with their girlfriend or wife. When I was going through a bad patch I was sitting on my own sniffing line after line, which I'm ashamed to admit.

I'd always mix it with alcohol. It's virtually fucking impossible not to, because one runs with the other. Throughout my cocaine addiction I was a full-blown alcoholic too. I've drunk more vodka than anyone in Russia. I'd easily get through three bottles a day, coked off my tits. The coke makes you so high that one reacts to the other.

The worst point of taking cocaine is when your body can't take any more. It shuts down and that's when the nightmare begins, because it's impossible to sleep. It's taken me a day to get to sleep, many times. Just to shut my eyes. Your heartbeat is going 6,000mph. Your feet are fucking sweating. You're rolling up and over, backwards and forwards, with horrific thoughts going through your mind. You're thinking about your parents and everything you've ever done wrong in your life. It's a dreadful experience. You're absolutely fucked and can't function, but you're too wired to sleep. I've tried everything to get my head down over the years. I took temazepam, aspirin and even paracetamol. I've never been a weed smoker, but I did try and smoke a bit to zonk me. It never worked, so I just kept on using cocaine.

Even if you're knackered, after a few lines coke takes you back to where you were before. "I'm all right now. I'm proper, I'm powerful," you lie to yourself. You can get back on it but eventually, no matter how much you take, there comes a point when you've got to stop. The end of the session, if it'd been a night or five days, was always horrible. I can remember trying to go to bed and still being wide awake 12 hours later. You physically can't sleep. The thoughts going through your mind are fucking terrible. You get flashbacks to you as a child. I used to pray to God: "Please get me through the night, and I'm going to clean myself up. I'm going to stop, this is it. I'm finished with it."

At the time you'd swear your life on it, but lo and behold, the next day comes and you're calling a bit more gear in. You say to yourself: "I'm only young. I've got a few bob. It's just an angle to escape." You're mugging yourself off, mate.

It steals *time* from you. You become a person that doesn't exist. Most people who use coke, when they're not using, are nice people. I was a bit of a young brash Jack the Lad, but I was always a very generous person. I helped people, and took time to speak to anyone. When you use coke you become a false identity.

A very good friend of mine called Steve, who is sadly no longer with us because of the drug, said to me one day: "Martin, why don't you leave it? You're a character in your own right. As soon as you hit that powder you change, you're a monster." It's true. It changes people, the way they look, their facial expressions. It's so likeable that weak-minded people who get hooked are in trouble because they might not pull through. I know three people, two of them very well, who have died after getting hooked on cocaine. Two of them took their own lives.

I've written this book to help people get off the gear, or warn those thinking about doing it to think twice. People need to know that there's no such thing as a part-time user. So-called social users are mugging themselves off. It's not only taking your money. Slowly but surely it will chip away at your personality. You will change. You will get very irritable through the week. If someone starts going out at the weekend and having a few lines with a drink, the addiction will quickly develop. It makes them become a different person. They think they're so powerful, and they just want more. They come out of their shell. They talk so fast that no one can keep up with them. If someone starts by taking one gram once a week, it will quickly become twice a week, and two grams. Slowly but surely, that creeps into the week. They go: "Fuck it, Wednesday night, I'll have a gram. I've had a shit day at work. Do you want to come round? I've got a bit of gear."

As time goes on you get more into the drug, because you like what it does to you. That's when the danger creeps in and the old cocaine man knocks on the door, and you can't say no. Most people crumble at this point, and it turns into a full-blown addiction. You start meeting other users, and moving in circles where the gear is always readily available. "Pay me at the end of the week," they say. Then you get into trouble and you get into debt. This is when the misery starts to kick in and you get people that have gone that far, and unfortunately some of them are fucked because they haven't got the determination to get off it. It's a never-ending story, and it escalates until they've lost their job, they're in debt, they look dreadful, their friends and family have parted with them, and they're now mixing with undesirable people, as I was myself. When you're at that stage you can get trapped, with no route out.

As your life falls apart, cocaine swoops in and gives you an escape. That's what happened to me. When you're that low you take the drug, in your mind expecting things to get better. For that split second they do. Your problems disappear, but then this is the horror story: once you run out of the powder, reality kicks in and the problems come back three times worse. Now, your only way of getting out of that is to use again.

When I was at my lowest point I was using as much as possible, for the simple reason that on the rare occasions I sobered up, I came up against fucking massive problems. Your wife has gone, your kids have gone, most of your wealth has gone, you look like shit, the feelings in your mind are so complicated that you can't think straight because you're so fuelled with the coke. What it boils down to is softening the blow by taking another line of coke. I got a slight rush with it, and for that brief moment my problems disappeared. I'd put a record on, and my problems would drift out of the window as I moved into this different world. I'd be rich again. "Everything's going to be great," I'd say to myself. But the real fact of the matter is that when you come off that cocaine buzz and the shit hits the fan, your problems are a million times worse. They're building up so quickly, you've got nowhere to turn. The only way for you to escape it is to use again – and that's why it's such a dangerous drug. You get hooked on it. You're relying on it, and using it for comfort. Trying to escape the reality of your problems whether it be your rent, your health or your wife. The list becomes endless.

I would say anyone that thinks using cocaine is going to help them further their business, their relationships, or just generally make them a more powerful or prominent person, has got it all wrong. It's completely the reverse. You'll lose everything, from the shirt on your back to your relationships. It doesn't take long. It will creep up on you very quickly.

That's why you don't get any happy endings with cocaine. It's always going to finish up with sadness, however the media glamourise it. As an ex-user I know there's only one way a coke-head is going, and that's in the gutter. And when you're in the gutter, it's fucking hard to get out. When people say to me "Is coke hard to get off?" I say it isn't hard to get off. Anyone can stop. But *maintaining* that is very difficult, because you're always clucking for a line. You're gagging for more. The cravings I had after my 30-odd-year run were horrific.

My thoughts on it are very anti-drug now, which is

unbelievable after so many years of using it. On TV they try and portray it as the thing to do. It's the trend – lines of coke go with scantily dressed women and fast cars. It's the champagne lifestyle. That's all bollocks, because at the end of it, all it does is ruin your life. There are no success stories in cocaine. Even if you look at people who were massive drug dealers, like Pablo Escobar, their lives end in tragedy. They're either shot or put in prison for the rest of their life.

I don't think the media have scratched the surface with cocaine. They need to put someone on TV on a six-month run to realise the dramas, the traumas and the sadness that cocaine can bring – to enlighten people, instead of sweeping it under the carpet.

Today things are worse than in my day. You've got young kids selling it on street corners. It's common knowledge, from East London to West One. Everyone knows cocaine exists, but it's getting worse. It's rancid. It's like a cancer, and it's spreading every day. If you go out into the suburbs and the countryside, it's there too. It's never going to go away. It needs to be brought to the attention of the public, because if we don't stop it then it's only going to get worse.

I hope that by writing this book I can educate people not to make the same mistakes I did, and stay well clear of the dreaded powder.

CHAPTER 1:

THE BEGINNING

THE BEGINNING

I was brought screaming into the world on October 22, 1963 at St Andrew's Hospital under the Bow Bells in East London. I was Mervin and Mary John's third child, and their first son to survive to adulthood. My sister Julie had arrived two years earlier. As their only son, I was undoubtedly their favourite, which caused issues with Julie over the years.

My first home was 18 Morgan Street in Bow, East London. The two-up, two-down terraced brick house is in a very trendy area these days. I went back there recently and the fella who answered the door said he'd just bought it for £900,000. When we lived there it was a fucking dreadful old Victorian slum that was decades from being gentrified. We rented it for £2 a week, and often my parents struggled to stump up even that modest amount. I remember it was always damp and bitterly cold. Most of the time there was no electric because we'd get cut off when Dad hadn't paid the bill. There was no TV or luxuries that people get these days. If you were lucky you'd be able to play with some marbles. We had an old Victorian outside toilet that was freezing.

It was like the terraced houses in Coronation Street that people remember nostalgically. They're all the fashion now, with their central heating and double glazing. Back then they were horrible. No one wanted to move there. It was in E3, the epitome of East London. It was rough and ready, and crammed full of very poverty-stricken families. We were fucking one of them, without a shadow of a doubt. It was very humble surroundings to grow up in, but you just did the best with what you could. We were so poor that my parents couldn't afford proper clothes, so I dressed in rags. Food was very basic too. There were no a la carte meals, I can assure you of that. In our house food was always there but when it was there it was there and if you missed it you were stuffed. It wasn't 6pm, "There's your egg on toast, love." That wasn't going to happen. There were no Sunday dinners with the family round the table at my house.

I had a very cold upbringing, both emotionally and physically. My parents loved me but they didn't show any affection. That just wasn't their way. Birthdays and Christmases didn't exist. I never had a Christmas tree at home until I was 27. We never had a single decoration in the house. I remember we'd regularly have beans on toast for Christmas dinner. To me that was normal. Celebrations just didn't exist in my family. I never had a holiday with my parents. Throughout my entire childhood we went out twice for a meal. Where most families go out for meals, my dad would say, "Fuck that old bollocks, we aren't doing all that old shit."

It was a very unusual childhood, and I think this stems from my parents' experiences as children. The pair of them didn't know how to express their emotions. They both had terrible, rough, poverty- stricken early lives. They literally had nothing. Not a pint of milk or a loaf of bread to their names. I suppose that rolled over in how they raised me and Julie.

My dad was a character in his own right and still is to this day, despite being an elderly pensioner. He was born in 1928 on a Welsh farm, in abject poverty. He couldn't even afford shoes on his feet. His family came to London when he was very young. They were so poor that he had to wear girls' clothes because they couldn't afford boys' ones. To this day I've got a picture with him wearing a little girl's smock thing.

My dad never saw eye-to-eye with his father, Arthur John. Arthur was what my dad called a 'straight' man. He was an honest, hard-working mechanic who never strayed off the straight and narrow. My dad was the complete opposite. He had no problem stealing something if he needed it. They never got on, especially when Mervin became notorious in Bow for causing trouble as a teenager. Arthur looked down on him. His mum Dolly used to look after my dad and try and hush things up when they lived in Malmesbury Road, Mile End.

Arthur gave my dad a hard time when he went into prison as a young man. I think that's where he got his temper from. Arthur never helped him. He resented that, and got a little chip on his shoulder. Most people would in that situation. A little bit of resentment and anger crept in, and has stayed with him to this day. In my experience, some people are just that way inclined to start with. Mervin definitely was, and his early life made things a thousand times worse. It made him an angry man, prone to lash out.

It's a terrible thing to call your own father, but Mervin was a wicked man. Fighting's never been my thing, but from what I've learnt and what I've seen, being a wicked man is a million times worse than being a good fighter. Being wicked makes a man unpredictable. You never know what's coming. Anyone can go outside and put their hands up. Wicked men will do wicked things. My father was fearless, and the only person he's ever been scared of is himself, because he's got such a chip on his shoulder.

Things got so bad at home with his dad that Mervin used to live downstairs with his mum, and Arthur was upstairs with his sister Myra. I'll never forget a story he told me about when they had a big falling-out. Mervin was a young man at this point, and his lorry wouldn't start. He asked his dad to have a look at it. When he said no, my father broke his ribs. He regretted that for the rest of his life. After that, Arthur disowned him.

They didn't see so much of each other anyway, because Mervin was always in and out of prison. Another time he beat up his brother-in-law Peter, who was also his cousin. Myra had married her own cousin. They were arguing non-stop over the years. One day he had a go at Myra, and my dad beat the fuck out of him. He ended up in hospital with serious injuries. It's a terrible thing, but that's just how it went.

My mother didn't have it any easier. She was born Mary Ruston in 1934 in Bow, into a very poor family. My dad was the local hoodlum in Bow. Her sister Renne died aged 29 from a brain haemorrhage. Her other sister Dott was an alcoholic who died at 40. Her family were beset by bad luck, and it deeply affected her.

My parents met as teenagers in Mile End Road, where my mother used to work in a petrol station. My dad pulled in one day and they hit it off from there. Most people got married in their early 20s in those days. My parents would have been no exception, but with my dad in prison all the time they had to wait until he was out long enough to arrange it. It wasn't until 1957, when they were 29 and 24 respectively, that Mervin managed to tie the knot. In their wedding photo my dad has got his hand behind his back, holding his jacket together because it's too big. He'd just got out of prison and couldn't afford one that fitted properly. My mum paid for the wedding because he was so skint.

They were married for 55 years in all. She stood by him through thick and thin, despite the years he spent in prison and the nightly rows they had when he was out. It caused very bad friction in the house. They'd often argue about my dad going out drinking. He'd come home, throw his dinner against the wall, and it would go off from there. It's not for me to say if it was a happy marriage, but things were different in those days. People didn't get divorced. Women were expected to stay with their husbands no matter what happened. My mother was a proud East End woman, and she certainly wasn't going to walk away from her marriage.

In his early days Mervin was what they used to call a hoodlum. He quickly progressed from petty street crime into bigger things in the 1950s, when the East End was full of gangsters. He was always causing trouble, and used to mix with a lot of undesirable characters. This behaviour carried on after my parents got together, and he was always involved in all sorts of criminality in his early life. My mother's side of the family didn't approve, and he had a very tenterhooks relationship with her sisters from day one.

Before I was born, Mervin was involved with a man called Johnny Squibb. He was a very close friend of the Kray twins, and later ran a multi-million-pound demolition company called Squibb and Davies, which exists to this day. My mother went out with Charlie Kray for three years before she met my dad, so she had a connection too.

One night Mervin got in a disagreement with the Krays after he apparently called Ronnie Kray a cunt in a pub. A while later he was drinking in another pub with his friend, Mackie Stevens – a bank robber from East London – and the Kray twins walked in. The pair of them ended up fighting the Krays and about ten of their mates. In the end, they cut his right cheek and lip with a knife. He's still got the scar to this day. He's always said to me: "I never won, but I never lost." In those days, the Krays weren't that well known, but he knew they could still cause him trouble. To avoid it he decided to go to Manchester with Mary, to get away from them.

He was running a nightclub with Johnny Squibb, but he tried to screw him over and extort money out of him. My dad wouldn't let him pull the wool over his eyes, so they parted company. He came back to London about a year later, looking to make a fresh start. One night he was having a meal in a Chinese restaurant in Mile End with my mum, and the Krays came in. He said: "Fuck it. I don't believe it. Ronnie and Reggie Kray just walked in." They came over and my mum picked up a carving knife. Ronnie said, "Mary, put that down. Don't be stupid." He then said: "Can we have a word with you Mervin?" They walked out with my dad and said: "You took a fucking liberty with us." He was expecting more trouble, but they just walked away. That's the last he ever saw of them. The next thing he knew, they'd be arrested and put away.

After that they settled back in Bow and managed to rent a house where Julie and I were born. Mervin was still going out causing trouble, and was involved in everything from fraud to assault. The courts took a dim view of his extensive criminal record and he was regularly sent down for three- to five-year stretches. This meant that until the age of six I never saw much of him. One of my earliest memories was around 1968, when I had an operation at St Andrew's Hospital because of a turn in my right eye. My dad came in to see me and gave me a fire engine. He said, "I've just nicked that from the toy shop on Roman Road." That was just how he was.

Another time I remember going to see him in Wormwood Scrubs when I was barely out of nappies. I sat on my mum's lap and spilt a cup of tea over his prison uniform, which was blue and white in those days. I can still vividly remember the tea tumbling out of the cup and turning his lap a darker shade of blue. I said, "What are you doing in here, Dad?" He said, "I'm working." I genuinely believed him. It was only years later that I realised why he was really there.

When he wasn't inside he was often on the run or up to some sort of mischief. I remember seeing him get arrested at our house in Bow when I was about four. A CID officer called Alan Player came around because my dad was on the run. Mervin saw him at the front door and said, "I'd better fuck off." He tried jumping over a brick wall round the back, but Mr Player ran through the house to the garden. He caught up with him and said, "Mervin you've got your son here, you can't let him see this." My dad stopped and gave himself up. Two more uniformed coppers came in and took him away. I didn't see him for another few years after that.

While he was in prison it would be just Mum, Julie and me at home. That went on for years, and seemed the norm growing up. When I turned five I was enrolled at Malmesbury Road Primary School, which was just down the road from the house. I hated it, and only went a handful of times before my mum pulled me out. There was a very different attitude to education in those days, and she didn't see the benefit of me going. The school didn't really chase her up about it, and it was only years later that truant officers caught up with me. I was happy staying at home at the time but the knock-on effect of that was that my reading and writing skills are very poor, even to this day.

As well as being violent, Mervin was a drinker. He used to drink Scotch like it was going out of fashion. It caused a lot of drama in my family, and made me a very timid boy growing up. Having a father like Mervin makes you very nervous, and I was always surviving on my wits. When I was young Mervin had a bad tempter, especially when he'd been drinking. He was a hardened man and the real deal, not like these plastic gangsters you see on TV. He put the fear in you. He did his best for me, but his own difficult upbringing didn't help the way he went about it. I had a very distant relationship with them both. Mervin was such a strong character that he never liked being challenged. One of his friends once to me: "He's one of the most unpredictable men I've ever known." He could change in a split second. He wasn't a psychopath but he was very unpredictable, which to me is dangerous. He would be all normal, but then you know he can go off at any minute. I never used to say anything, and it made it very difficult to get through each day, thinking something's going to happen. All the time I'd be thinking there's going to be a row indoors. The mood swings were up and down – and it was a hundred times worse when he'd been to the pub. Unpredictable people: one minute they're fine, the next they're not.

People are coming in and out the house, most of them undesirables. Not necessarily bad people, and I wouldn't be the man I am today without meeting these people, but as a young child it's nerve-wracking. If Mervin came home from the pub and he'd had a drink, you'd have to be fucking worried. You'd go into your room and hope there's no shouting and screaming going on because he'd thrown his dinner out of the window.

His temper would get to a very high level very quickly. I remember seeing my sister and mother on the floor rolling about with him. He wouldn't think twice about using his hands to give you a whack. As a child you wouldn't dare to ask what was for dinner. You'd be taking your life in your own hands. You're fucking joking. You aren't going to do that. You'd be asking for trouble. Be grateful for what you got, and eat it. Whenever my friends used to come round I used to tell them: "Whatever you do, don't say anything to my dad. Don't talk. Don't start him off, because he'll go into one." He could turn at any minute, and then there's going to be mayhem to pay. There's going to be murders. When my sister went out I used to change the clock so he thought she was getting in earlier. He said, "Be in by 9pm." I used to put it back a couple of hours because I was shitting myself that he'd go into one if he thought she was late.

Growing up, she really had a problem with him. It went on for years. She used to say to me, "Mum and dad always take your side." It's a sad thing to say, but it's a hundred per cent true. I love my sister dearly and speak to her all the time now, but back then we had a very strained relationship. She went through a lot of shit, and was jealous because I was the favourite. I've never discussed that with her because it's a very sore point, but it was true.

To be fair to her, she used to stand her ground. She'd row with my dad all the time. She wouldn't give a fuck. She'd stand up to protect my mother. Shouting and screaming at him when he was getting in late. Julie never missed a drama. I think that's why she wasn't close to him later on in life. I kept my nut down, so to speak, but when we got older it turned out that later in life I would be the rascal, and shine, and come through. I came out of poverty and actually made it.

Now, the tables have completed turned. I always thought my childhood experiences were the reason why later on in life I got wrapped up in cocaine. It's because I wanted to escape. I don't want to come up with excuses, but it explains a lot.

Despite all his faults, I've got to say Mervin's principles were unbelievable. He'd never see you without anything. If you didn't have a pound, he'd give it to you. I remember when my mum's sister Reene was upstairs in bed, dying from a brain haemorrhage. Her sons were downstairs with no coal, practically freezing to death. At the time, my dad did a coal round. He nicked half of it. He used to sell it straight off the lorry, and then scarper before he could get caught. Reene was so ill she couldn't look after the kids.

They were downstairs, no food, and with snotty noses. My dad used to give them coal and anything else they needed to get by. He did a lot more than Lesley Tucker, Reene's husband. He was a lazy fucker who couldn't give a toss about his wife or family. One day my dad went into the pub in Barking and beat the fuck out of him. He deserved it. The woman's dying, and he's in the pub laughing and joking.

My dad was a drinker, but he wasn't all bad. He was a hard man to function with, and you couldn't argue with him because you'd be in trouble, but he had his principles and he stuck by them. As time went on Dad gradually calmed down and stopped his cycle of offending. He turned his attention to making money in more legitimate ways. He might not have been academic, and he couldn't read or write, but he's the cleverest man I've ever met, and he knew how to make a pound note.

His first business was selling toffee apples. My mother's got a bit of a connection with fairground people and showmen. She would spend hours at home boiling up all the ingredients to cover the apples with, and then we'd go around the streets selling them in dad's old Bedford TK lorry for 1p a pop. It was fucking horrible and I hated doing it, not that I had much choice. I used to ring the bell and shout "toffee apples" endlessly, all around the roughest parts of London and the South East. It was a terrifying experience for a timid little boy.

As soon as they were all sold my parents used to go into the pub. Me and Julie would have to sit in the lorry with a little bottle of lemonade. We'd go all over selling them. Once we even went to Southend-on-Sea in Essex, where I bought a little policeman's hat with some pocket money. I loved that hat, and used to wear it all the time. A short while later we were selling the toffee apples in

Canning Town and a kid punched me in the mouth. He said, "We don't like policeman around here." My dad laughed and said, "You learnt a fucking lesson there." I was only about seven, but I'll never forget it.

By the time he came out of prison for the last time, the house in Morgan Street was falling apart and wasn't a fit place for a young family to live in. Dad was struggling to pay the rent. His prison governor gave Mervin a letter, which he handed over to the council. They ended up offering us a two-bed flat to live in on the Isle of Dogs.

Back then, the Isle of Dogs was a shithole. It wasn't like it is now with Canary Wharf, full of hipsters with beards. It was a very rough area, and the docks were still in use. I remember seeing the boats and barges coming and going. If you said you were from there, people used to say, "I wouldn't want to live there." Originally we moved into number 74 on the 19th floor, in a place called Bow Spirit Point on West Ferry Road. It was a brand spanking new council flat back then. After a few years there we got a swap and moved to number 81, the penthouse suite on the 21st floor. It's worth £820,000 today. My dad got it through the right to buy for £11,000 in the 1980s.

The surroundings might have been better, but the move didn't stop my dad drinking. That meant there was always tension in that flat, and my parents were arguing constantly. The older Julie got, the more she used to argue with him, which made things even worse. If he'd been out and he came back in a mood, there was going to be trouble. My mum was still doing her best, but it was a very meagre existence.

The trouble at home didn't stop things picking up business-wise. When I turned eight, Mervin stopped selling toffee apples and started getting into scrap metal. We'd spend most days going out looking for scrap on the lorry. That's why I never went to school. I was always out working with my dad. When I was ten a truant officer come around asking where I was. My old man gave him a bit of verbal, and that was the end of that. I never went to school after that. I think they gave up in the end.

For all his faults, Mervin was very capable of earning money. In East London they called that a 'money-getter'. You were either a 'straight man' or a 'money-getter'. Mervin was a top-class money-getter, there's no doubt about that. The sad thing is, he drank it all. He did scrap metal when no one ever did it, and he made a lot of money. He was always about, and had his fingers in several pies at a time. Not all of it was crooked business, but he mixed in those circles. A lot of deals went down.

He had a very good contract with a company called the Fred Olsen Line. He was getting containers full of stuff bought in through the docks that he was flogging on. He had tonnes and tonnes of gear that was worth good money. I remember once he had rolls of newspaper paper. It's called pulp. There was a paper company in Bow called Davidson's that he was selling it to. He had a good business with them and it was ticking over smoothly until he fucked it all up because he got drunk and didn't turn up. Another time he had a contract with a few hospitals, running their nurses to work through a cab office he had in Chancery Lane, Holborn. He had about three or four cars running and it was a good business until he fucked it up, drinking and not turning up.

No matter what he did, he always went back to scrap metal. He was really on to something, because it was very lucrative. He'd take me out in the lorry and we'd drive around London looking for scrap. We'd go everywhere, from Chelsea to Hackney. We spent a lot of time up the West End, Battersea and Embankment. That's why I know London so well. We'd go down every street looking for scrap, asking anyone if they'd got anything. It taught me invaluable people skills.

My dad would get me to jump out of the lorry and talk to people. Obviously, it's embarrassing at the start because people tell you to fuck off. But whether it be a factory or a shop, he taught me to go in and say, "Excuse me, sir, have you got any old junk or old scrap that you want to get rid of?" Most people used to ring the bell and wait but my dad taught me to go in and talk to people, that way you're far more likely to be successful. He used to pull up on the side of the road and I'd do the whole street.

It was a unique way of getting stuff. Most people go looking for scrap lying around on the street. But when you go into a shop, most people have stuff out the back they want rid of. You can get some amazing stuff that way. I remember I once got an old antique cartwheel in one place, and a load of old-fashioned brass cash tills in another.

What I gathered from that had a massive part to play later on in my life, when I was a wealthy man. It made me very sharp, not just regarding wheeling and dealing: it made me realise that it's not impossible to make money if you're switched on.

Going in and out of the shops asking for scrap metal was embarrassing at a young age. I was only around eight when I started doing it. Sometimes you used to get a bit of flak off people who would tell you to clear off, but it also worked a lot of the time. We'd go everywhere asking for things. I remember walking into a garage and asking, "Have you got any exhausts you want to get rid of, sir?" I'd go into supermarkets too, and ask if they had anything lying around that they wanted to get rid of.

It was amazingly successful. I'd say back in those days, 50 per cent of the time you would get something. That experience made you get old very quickly. By the age of 12 I was like a man of 20. You had to fend for yourself. It did give me a fantastic insight into street life, and it's made me the man I am today. It was priceless knowledge: you weren't going to get that in school or college.

On an average day we'd head out early in the morning, and normally have loaded up the lorry by 1pm. After that it was back to a scrapyard in Bow called Yallops, or other one in Canning Town called Goodwins. We used to go on the weighbridge and get paid cash. I'd get a couple of quid off my dad if I was lucky, and then it was straight off to the pub. I'd sit in the lorry for hours while he was in the pub. Then we'd drive home after he'd finished and he'd have a row with my mum. That was an everyday occurrence for years, unless he had a hangover or didn't go out, or he'd already had a row with her.

CHAPTER 2

—

GOLF

The daily routine of going to pubs after weighing in the scrap went on for years. Mervin would take me to pubs all over London after we'd sold whatever scrap we'd found. As I got a bit older he used to let me go inside rather than sit in the lorry. This led to me meeting one of his good friends, an ex-crook called 'Fat' Freddie Clarke, who was well known in the East End. He was a lovely big fat geezer who owned a pub in Mile End called The Aberdeen where they used to do live music. It's been knocked down now, but it was right by Victoria Park. We went in there one day when I was 12. Freddie was chatting away when he said to me, "You ought to start playing a bit of golf." He gave me a couple of old clubs he'd bought from a second-hand shop, and sent me on my way.

A few days later I made a point of going down to a pitch and putt on Lea Bridge Road, Leyton. There was still a lot of grief at home, and I did it for the simple reason that I could get away from it. I didn't think it would come to much, but it turned out I was very good at it. It was also an escape route to get away from problems at home. I can say with all honesty that it was the first thing I ever enjoyed.

From the pitch and putt I quickly progressed to playing on an 18-hole course at Hainault Forest Golf Club in Romford. Over the next three years I played relentlessly. Every spare minute I had I'd be there, practising and perfecting my techniques. The minute we got in from collecting scrap I'd go and play. I still wasn't going to school and the truant officer got wind that I was always at the golf club after someone grassed me up. He came over one time looking for me. I was in the changing rooms and John the caddymaster said, "Watch out, he's after you." I was hiding and I heard them talking. John didn't say anything and the bloke left empty-handed.

Over the next two years my golfing skills came on in leaps and bounds. When I was 14 I shot a round of 67. By the age of 15 I'd got down to a handicap of one. They put it on the board as the best round of golf by a child. It's never been known there, and it's still never been beaten there. At Hainault they called me Millwall because I was from E14. I was such a character down there that if you went over to the clubhouse now they'd remember me. Because it was a bit posh and I was a youngster from a working-class area, some of the older guys used to give me a bit of stick. There was a man in there who was taking the piss out of me because I was from the Isle of Dogs. I'd taken my dad down there with his mate to watch me play that day. He turned around and said to the bloke: "Come outside and I'll break your neck." He shit himself, and never said a word to me after that.

When I first started playing golf on a regular basis my father encouraged me. But when I started playing more and more he got the hump. It got to the point when I was playing golf more than I was working, and he was getting annoyed. I was doing well for myself, and a little bit of jealousy crept in.

It wasn't to last, though. At the age of 16 I managed to get a job at Chigwell Golf Club in Essex as an assistant pro. It was supposed to be the start of my new career, but I only lasted a day. I'll never forget when I walked into the clubhouse. The course's professional, Eddie Whitcomb, was there. He was old-school, and hated when people broke the club's strict dress code. He said to me, "Martin John, you aren't coming in here with a pair of jeans on." Being a gobby little shit, I told him to fuck off and he sacked me on the spot. I was only there a few hours, and it was probably the biggest mistake of my life. If I'd carried on doing it I might have had an opportunity in my life.

After that my golf fizzled out, which is a tragedy that I regret to this day. If I'd carried it on I could have been very wealthy through it. I could have done something with myself. I'm saying that from the bottom of my heart. If I'd kept my nut down I would have had a chance of turning professional because I know I had the talent. I say that sincerely. It's a natural thing, and you've either got it or you haven't. The professional at Hainault was called Ron Frost, who later sadly died after he had a nervous breakdown. He encouraged me and said I could go all the way but I let it go, which is my own fault.

After I was sacked from Chigwell I went back to playing at Hainault. We used to play a little speed round on Wednesday morning. It was a £1 sweep and I used to win it all the time. I was still good, but I'd lost the drive to keep pushing myself. I didn't have that desire to keep on trying to improve.

As the golf fizzled out I spent more time with my dad on the lorries. We started moving into the West End, looking for scrap and contacts. We hit the jackpot on one occasion when I was 17. I went into a big building just off Sloane Street in Chelsea called Chelsea Choristers. It's still there – it's been turned into luxury flats. As we drove past I saw an old cast-iron radiator outside. My dad said, "Go in and ask if they've got anything." I went into the office at the front and a bloke came out called Mr Harrington. He said, "It might be your lucky day, young man."

We were there six months clearing it out. There were 800 flats in total and we cleared everything. I even found letters addressed to Lord Lucan, one of the building's tenants. Stupidly I threw them away, not knowing what they were worth.

The building was a gold mine, and we made a lot of money out of it. On the first day Mr Harrington took us up to the first floor in this old-fashioned lift. He showed us one of the flats and said, "This is the first room I want you to clear out." I remember it was crammed full of small cookers and table- top fridges. He said, "You can have all of them. Take them to start with." We sold them all in Holloway Road for about £300 that day. I couldn't believe it. We spent the next six months clearing out every single room. We took out the carpets, the curtains, and even the bedding. We had three lorry-loads of curtains, duvets and blankets. They'd all been dry cleaned and had never been unwrapped. I remember they still had the dry-cleaning bills attached. We sold every single one of them at a Hackney boot sale. They were selling so fast my mother ended up flogging them off the back of the lorry.

The flats had been built for aristocrats and were full of 1930s luggage. We got two lorry-loads of the stuff. I later sold it all to 20th Century Fox for film props. I jokingly told the bloke I sold it to about the Lord Lucan letters. He couldn't believe it, and said they would have been worth thousands, even in those days. I was kicking myself for weeks after that, and still to this day wonder how much they were worth. Luckily the letters weren't my only find. When we were in the basement I found three Rolexes lying about. Two of them had a leather strap, and the other one was stainless steel with no strap. I flogged them all down the Chelsea Arcade for £600. It was 1980, and that wasn't a bad price for them back then. They're probably worth more than ten times that now.

Making money off that building inspired my dad to find ways of making more cash. He did that by opening his own yard and buying in non-ferrous metals like copper, lead, zinc and aluminium. That's when we started making a lot more money.

It was good in some ways, but it took me away from the golf even more. Mervin didn't want to pay to rent a yard. For him that was a waste of money. Back in the early 1980s there were still a lot of old disused bomb sites in London. No one knew who owned them, and they just sat there. What he used to do was break the lock off one and put a caravan in it. From then on it was 'the yard'. We used to squat there, for years sometimes, before anyone said anything. Half the time no one knew who owned the ground anyway. We had one in Whitehorse Lane, then another in Commercial Road.

One day a bloke walked in and said, "Is this your yard?" I thought he was from the council so I lied and said it was. It was rammed full of scrap metal, car spares and a shop at the time. It turned out he was from a film studio, and wanted to do some filming in a scrapyard. I let them rent it out for £400 for the morning. They cordoned it all off so they could bring in catering lorries and all their equipment. The bloke starring in the show was Jim Broadbent, who went on to play Roy Slater in *Only Fools and Horses*. I couldn't believe what I'd just blagged. I remember me and a couple of my skulldugger mates were having bacon and egg sandwiches out of the catering vans while they were filming.

Eventually we found out that the land belonged to the council. We'd been there for two years when they came round and tried to kick us off. We tried to rent it off them and we nearly got it, but then they told us to clear off. When we refused they got the Sheriff of London to evict us. After that we used to rent yards for next to nothing, about £30 a week. We moved about a bit until we settled on a yard in Katherine Road, Forest Gate, where we started turning over half-decent money. There was very little regulation in the scrap metal industry in those days. You could just turn up, rent the place, put a set of scales in and away you go.

It's very simple, and money would come in straightaway. That apprenticeship helped me become a very wealthy man later on in life.

I was getting very well educated regarding not going out looking for scrap, but buying it in. I've still got a set of half a tonne Avery scales from those days. That's one thing I kept. As the yard took off we started making a lot more money.

I remember buying the metal in for cash and then running it down into a company in Rainham called F J Church and Sons, which is still there. When you went down there with a full lorry-load it could be worth anything from £1,500 to £3,000, depending on how much and what sort of metal you had. This meant that even though my dad was keeping most of it, he still paid me a few hundred pounds a week. That wasn't bad for an 18-year-old in 1981. That extra cash meant I could venture about more.

To get away from all the rowing at home I started getting out and about with my best friend Steve, who has since passed away. We started hitting the clubs in London. I don't know if that was the start of the cocaine addiction, but I was spending money and the women factor crept in. It progressed from there. I spent as much time out as I could because my dad was hard work, especially when he'd had a drink. The atmosphere at home wasn't great, so I didn't want to be there. I wanted my own space. I wanted to escape so I found my route by going out at least three times a week, as you do when you're young.

I was always seeing lots of girls. I never had one for a long period of time. They just came and went, but I remember quite a few of them – for good reasons and bad. One that sticks in my mind is Sarah Westwood. Her brother was Gary 'Snakehips' Westwood – an underworld enforcer suspected of killing ten people. He was very well connected. Their dad was gangland boss Alfie Westwood, killer of Frank 'Mad Axeman' Mitchell. He was a huge bloke who could apparently lift a full-size snooker table on his back. The Krays had got him out of prison, but had him killed when they couldn't control him.

Alfie did it. They shot him 12 times before he died. It all came about after they broke him out of prison and put him with an old brass in Barking Road, East Ham. He started getting a bit irritable, wanting to see them, and was threatening all sorts. Eventually they said, "He's got to go. He's become a liability." They got him in the back of van and shot him five times, but he still didn't die. The last shot was behind the ear-hole, apparently.

When I was 17 I went out with his daughter for a couple of months. She was a pretty blonde girl, but a fucking lunatic. I got on all right with her because we had similar backgrounds. She was a rough- and-ready girl. It was never going to be a ring with flowers though, we both knew that. Her dad was dead by that time. I think he died on the run. His son, Nicky Westwood, got murdered in Canning Town not long after we split up. I never met Nicky, but he mixed with undesirables to say the least. She had a weird upbringing. Her mum went a bit mad, for obvious reasons. She ended up with another skulldugger after me. We weren't together long, but it was long for me in those days. I remember I started to get itchy feet after a couple of months and bang, I moved on to the next girl.

CHAPTER 3

—

MY FIRST LINE

Just after I turned 18 I had my first experience with cocaine. It was at the Katherine Road yard with Steve, and it totally blew me away. I had no idea at that point what it was going to do to my life. We were upstairs in the flat and he said he had some. I'd heard about cocaine, as drugs were about in those days, but they were nowhere near as common as they are now. I remember being apprehensive about taking it. I nearly turned it down because I was worried about what it might do to me. But then I thought, "I didn't have a great upbringing, fuck it, I'll have some."

I tried it, and immediately it made me feel great. I'd never experienced anything like that before. I felt like a new man, under starter's orders. I could do anything. No one could stop me. I was the man. We only had about half a gram between the two of us, but it lasted us for hours. We felt amazing in that flat, buzzing our tits off. It was an unreal experience, and after that I couldn't wait to try it again. I never knew it at the time, but it was the start of my nightmare. I always think to myself, if I'd said no, maybe my life would have been a completely different story. Maybe I wouldn't have been on a 30-year journey as an addict.

My cocaine addiction didn't escalate to start off with. It was still under control at this point. I remember during my late teens and early 20s I never made a point of buying coke. I could go out without taking it, but slowly it crept into my life more and more. It went from the odd occasion on a night out to something I would expect and look forward to every time I went out. Because I was still going out a lot, it made my usage go up very quickly. Even though I didn't know it, I was already on the road to addiction.

A few months after I had my first line I bumped into Julie Davey, who was to become my first serious girlfriend. She would later be a property magnate, worth millions of pounds as founder of the Angel Group. When I met her she was a 27-year-old bunny girl at the Playboy Club, who still lived with her six sisters in Leytonstone. Her family were originally from Harrogate in Yorkshire, and moved down to London to make their fortune. We met in a pub called the Charleston when I caught her eye with my unusual dress sense. As a young man I always prided myself on having a bit of style, and I'd frequently go into London and buy some unusual clothes to stand out amongst the crowd. I introduced myself and she said, "You're very smart, you've got style."

We cracked it straight off and when we kissed I thought I'd hit the jackpot.

I was only 18, but our relationship kicked off very quickly and she soon met my mum and dad. My mum's first words were: "You're a lot older than my son." Julie's reply, in her northern accent, was "You're a cheeky bastard." Even though she connected with my dad, she thought he was hard work and she didn't like the way he spoke to my mum or me.

After six months, I moved into her flat with her sisters. That was great fun, as you can well imagine. We spent the next two and a half years together and had a great time. I really connected with Julie because we were both ambitious and wanted to make sometimes of ourselves. I liked the fact that she wasn't scared of hard work. She was a pretty girl and would get all dolled-up, but she didn't mind coming out on the scrap lorries either. Sometimes she'd bring her brother Magnus along. We got on well and he used to do a bit of work for me in those days. He's a multi-millionaire now, who owns a company called Docklands Estate Agents. He later said to me, "When I was a young kid, you educated me."

A year after I moved into her house we got a flat together

through a housing trust on the Isle of Dogs, because I had a connection there through my parents. That could have been our first step to starting a family and settling down but, as usual, I fucked it up. I was still a young man at that point and had a wandering eye. Much to my later regret, I was mucking around with another woman. Julie found out and we finished the relationship straightaway. When it was over she said, "Martin, I'll buy you out of the house." She gave me £2,000 and kept the flat. That was her first property. Years later, she is one of the richest women in England.

After we broke up I didn't see her for years. I still used to think about her, but I thought it was goodbye forever until 1987, when a friend of mine said she wanted to contact me. I called her on one of those big old-fashioned mobiles phones that weighed about two stone. The first thing she said to me was: "I want to see you, you bastard." We agreed to meet at Mile End Station. I got the train there and she turned up in a dark blue Mercedes SL500. Instead of exchanging pleasantries she just said, "Get in, you bastard", and laughed. We went to a pub in Burdett Road called Inn on the Park, which has been knocked down now.

When we were inside she gave me £2,000 in a big brown envelope. She said, "That's for you. I've done well for myself." I was shocked, but I didn't turn the money down. We've been great friends ever since, and still speak to this day.

After splitting up with Julie I divided my time between the flat in Forest Gate and my parents. They were constantly arguing, and I just wanted to get away from it. Cocaine was my angle to escape. I was constantly going out and started getting coke off this bloke called Brian. He ran a market stall up in Old Street. We used to go clubbing in the West End and got on the gear several times a week. We'd go out every Friday, Saturday and Sunday to places like Rah Rah's. It was pretty rough and ready up there, but the music was good and gear was always on tap. On Mondays, we'd head to Stringfellow's for the celebrity night. It was guest-list-only, but I knew one of the doormen who used to let us in. The coke was rancid in there, you could do it at the bar and no one would care.

Brian was a happy-go-lucky sort of guy and we connected. We had a good laugh, but it wasn't to last. A couple of months after we started going clubbing together he got murdered. He got into a dispute with someone over a drug debt, so they smashed him over the head with a hammer in Old Bethnal Green Road. It should have been a wake-up call, but if anything my intake went up.

Steadily my consumption got higher and higher. Instead of it being an occasional treat, it became the norm. Every time I went out I had coke. The time flew by in a haze of drugs and alcohol. It got to the stage where I was spending £200 a week on the stuff. That's a lot, considering a gram was about £30 back in the early '80s. Wild nights on the booze turned to heavy nights on the coke. I thought I had it under control, but I couldn't have been more wrong.

CHAPTER 4

—

MY FIRST CHILD

It is a terrible thing to say, but I became a father entirely by accident and I wasn't ready for it. I was cruising through my 20s, going out all the time and getting more into coke, when I met Sharon. I was 22 and still working with my dad. He was giving me grief about going out drinking up the West End. It was a bit rich coming from him, but to get away from it I spent a lot of time living in the flat above the scrapyard in Forest Gate. With not a lot to do there I used to go out and mingle as I got more and more into the gear.

I'd only recently split with Julie when I met Sharon. She wasn't the typical type of girl I used to go for. She was a bit plump, and wasn't into going out and getting drunk. She wouldn't dream of taking cocaine or going on a four-day bender. She wanted to settle down and have a family. Maybe that's what attracted me to her. She was a quiet woman who'd been desperately trying to get pregnant for years. She was with someone before for ten years before we met, and they'd never managed to have a baby. They ran a clothes shop and were still in business together for the whole two years we were seeing each other. She was still working every day with her ex-fella throughout our on-off relationship. It didn't make me jealous, because I'm not the type, but I thought it was a bit weird. I wanted to get away from my dad so badly that I moved in with her pretty much immediately. I think it was an excuse to go around and find myself. Experience different things and cut loose, so to speak.

I quickly realised that the relationship wasn't going to happen. I moved in far too quickly and we didn't connect. I remember packing all my stuff in a little Ford truck and taking it round to her house in South Woodford. Very quickly I realised we didn't click. She just wasn't for me. I still wanted to be a single man and put myself about, so I decided to move on.

Before I could make my excuses and leave, she told me she was pregnant. I thought "Fucking hell. What I am going to do? I'm not ready to become a father." My mother insisted that I stay the course for the baby's sake. I tried, but I couldn't deal with her. We weren't in love, and there was no point us staying together and both being unhappy. It would have been a miserable existence for all concerned. It was a shock to me when the baby was born. She was called Charlie – a word that would come back to haunt me.

Shortly after she was born I told Sharon it was over, and we parted ways. I'm not sad about that, because sometimes you've got to be cruel to be kind. She wasn't very happy about it, to say the least. It was a difficult time for me, which meant I turned to cocaine even more. I was juggling trying to see the baby, running the scrap business and dealing with my parents' aggro.

Even after the split I was still determined to see Charlie. Unfortunately, Sharon made it nearly impossible. We ended up having to go to court, and had social services round to assess us. I remember this social worker interviewed my whole family and made out that he was on my side. He told me everything was going to be OK and I'd get access – even if it was supervised. I was happy with that, and believed him at the time. But when we went to Barkingside family court it all fell apart. Sharon told the judge she'd moved out of South Woodford so the case was out of his jurisdiction, which meant it had to start all over again.

Then, to add salt to my wounds the social worker stood up and said, "I've looked into the man's background. His family's rough. They're dodgy scrap-metal merchants. They've got Rottweiler dogs. His dad's an ex-criminal. He's not suitable to look after a young child." I was fuming. He'd lied to my face. He said he was going to be on my side, and now he's gone all pear-shaped on me.

Outside in the foyer I couldn't control my rage and headbutted him, knocking his two front teeth out. I'm not normally like that, but we've all got a limit. The ushers had to come over and break it up. If it happened again today I'd do the same thing. That day was the last time I ever saw Sharon, and the last time I saw Charlie for over 20 years.

After the judge's ruling my mother said, "You better leave it, if she wants to contact you when she's older she will." I took that advice. I didn't have much choice because I had no idea where she was, but it's affected our relationship. We are in contact sometimes but we're not close, which is a shame because we're the same blood.

As soon as I moved out I was back up the West End several times a week, letting my hair down and getting drunk and coked-up. I wasn't bothered about ending things with Sharon, but we had a kid together and I wanted to see Charlie. That wasn't possible, and as always I turned to the powder to get over things. Getting in the clubs on the trumpet, I met a lot of women. A lot of them were on gear too. Even though I was on the gear I was still holding it together at this point. I was coming up the ranks, meeting more and more people. I started to make more money with the shop in Forest Gate. I was basically running it by then, and it was making good money some weeks. I had that desire to succeed. I didn't know what was possible back then, so I kept striving to make more money and be someone. At that point I didn't know how I was going to do it. I was still very much focused on the scrap. But running that shop improved my people skills, and taught me how to strike up deals with people and haggle.

That was to come into great use later on in life, when I was buying furniture in bulk.

CHAPTER 5

—

MY FIRST SHOP

Over the next two years I spent my days running the shop, and my evenings and weekends pissing away every penny I earned from selling scrap on coke and booze.

Just after I turned 27, a woman walked into the yard and changed my life forever. It never occurred to me at the time quite how much. She said, "Do you take old furniture? I've just moved my son and daughter out of a house, and I've got a few of bits of pine. Will you take them?" I said no. She said, "Well, will you have a look?" I remember it was a wardrobe, a chest of drawers and a bedside table that looked quite nice, but nothing special. I agreed to take them but said I couldn't pay her anything. She was happy with that, so I put them in the yard, all the time thinking we'd have to get rid of them somehow.

Within hours of them being there I had people asking me how much they were. The number of people asking me was unbelievable, so I said they were for sale. They quickly went for about £150, which in itself I couldn't believe. After we sold them my dad said, "You might be on to something there. It might be worth seeing if you can buy any more from somewhere."

To investigate further I visited Hackney Road, which at the time was the main core of the wholesale furniture business in London. They sold all sorts around there, including a lot of reproduction furniture. On the road, I came across two pine wardrobes standing outside a little unit. I went inside and came across an old character called Tommy. He ran a company called T&K Pine. He was an old-school East Ender like my father, so we connected. I had a look around, then went on my way. For some odd reason I didn't want to take it up straightaway and I left it for a few months. Maybe I was scared to make a jump into the unknown.

Finally, I decided to take the plunge when I was out and about in Crouch End with Steve and my dad. By chance we spotted a small empty shop in Tottenham Lane. It had a little 'for rent' advert in the window. I took the number down and rang the landlord, who was called Oliver. All he said to me was "The shop's £60 a week", so I took it. When I told my dad, he wasn't overly struck because he was thinking I wouldn't carry on going to look for the scrap or buy the metal in.

I managed to get a couple of weeks' rent down, which wasn't easy because I was always spending money like it was going out of fashion. I decided to call the shop Strike It Lucky because that's what I thought I'd done. I went down to T&K Pine and bought a couple of bits of furniture. The shop was very bare so I put them in the window and taped the price on the side. It was the same evening that I got the keys, so they weren't even in there 24 hours and I was getting calls. My phone didn't stop ringing. It was astonishing – I couldn't believe it. I sold those three bits of furniture immediately so I went back to T&K Pine and replaced them, but they were selling faster than I could manage.

Within six weeks I went from selling two bits of furniture to taking £2,000 a week, which was a lot of money in those days. I was astonished, and so was my father. People were coming from everywhere, from every angle, just to buy furniture. I was doing two lorry-loads a day because I couldn't get enough furniture. The demand was so high that T&K Pine didn't have enough stock. Soon the shop couldn't fit enough furniture in to meet demand.

Around this time, I noticed that across the road there was a massive corner shop. It was a Poundland-type shop that was selling cheap old junk. Luckily for me it wasn't doing too well, and had just shut. I quickly rang the landlord up, who was an

Orthodox Jew called John. He said the rent was £120 a week, so I took it on the spot. It was massive, like three shops in one. I remember when we moved in I couldn't fill it up, even though I was taking thousands every week.

In the second shop, which I also called Strike It Lucky, I was taking £5,000 a week. It got so busy that I had to take on two staff. One of them was a Texan in his early 40s called Richard, who lived in the flat above the shop. He was an odd guy who came to London after he got into some trouble in the States. He'd spent a few years in American jails for drugs offences, and was on his last strike. He didn't want to get locked away for good, so he came to the UK. His dad was Scottish so he could stay here indefinitely. That's what he told me, anyway: I was never sure how much to believe. He was a character, that's for sure.

Another character who worked for me was a gentleman who bought a couple of bedside tables off me. He was a likeable and bubbly bloke called Irish Mark, for obvious reasons. After he'd bought some stuff I said, "I've got a bit of work, if you fancy it?" He agreed, and we struck up a close friendship over the next two decades. He was a nice, tight, good man, and came from seeing me have one shop to having dozens. He was always on board, no matter how hard things got. He was a heavy drinker and drug user, but a good man. We parted ways eventually because I stopped taking drugs, and I had to cut people who did out of my life.

When the second shop started really taking off we turned the original Strike It Lucky shop into a store room, just to keep up with demand. It was rammed full of furniture. I was out buying every day, but we were forever going back to Hackney Road to buy more.

It didn't feel real, making all that cash, and it was a very unusual experience. Even though I was in the non-ferrous metal business with my dad, money was scarce. It came in dribs and drabs. It would come, and be spent very quickly. With the shops it was a constant flow of money, and it was something I actually enjoyed. It was an escape route as well. Even though I was at a young age, I knew I had a little bit of a gift at selling things and making money. I didn't really know how quickly that would develop and flourish later on in life.

It was a weird experience, because I'd never been used to that kind of money. I remember the first purchase I ever made that stood out in my mind and made me choke up was a Rolex watch. I bought a two-colour stainless and gold Rolex watch from a man in Surrey called Lester for £2,500. I saw it in a paper called the *Loot* that was full of free classified adverts. To start with I was a bit reluctant to buy it, because it was a lot of money and I was worried it would be a fake. But after doing my research, and having large amounts of cash burning a hole in my pocket, I decided to go for it. It was a treat for myself that I felt I deserved after working so hard.

That was to be my first of many extravagant purchases. Within seven months I bought a brand-new Porsche 911 Turbo for £29,000 cash. I'd always loved Porsches since being a very young boy, and driving around in one made me feel like a king. It was 1990, and I was living the high life. I was making so much money that I stopped working with my dad and focused solely on the furniture business. Things were really kicking off, and I was loving life. I loved how my new-found wealth made me feel.

Another thing that made me feel better was cocaine. I was going out at least four nights a week, and every time I'd get on the coke. Having that amount of money meant I had no issue spending on coke, and there was a ready supply of that in London. Much like George Best: the rest went on booze, birds and fast cars.

CHAPTER 6

—

MEETING KAREN

I'd known Karen for years before we got together, but it never came to anything. She ran a pie and mash shop in East London which I used to go into on a regular basis. She was an attractive blonde and had a bubbly personality, so it didn't take rocket science to see why I liked her. She wasn't the doom and gloom which I'd had most of my life. After going through everything with Sharon and the baby, I missed having fun. We had a laugh and a joke with Karen, and nothing was ever too serious. After she caught my eye, it seemed like I was going into her shop every day. She felt the same, so we quickly hit it off and started seeing each other.

As with most relationships, it started off fairly casually but got serious pretty quick. Very soon after we'd met, she started inviting me round on a regular basis for dinner at her flat in Buckhurst Hill. For a lot of people that would be totally normal, but coming from my household I thought it was weird. For me it was very strange to come home and have food on the table waiting for me. I'd never experienced anything like that before. I remember saying to her, "You're making dinner for 6pm. What's all that about? I get in when I get in." I had never been brought up to have a routine like that.

Despite finding it strange, I liked it. It was a normal existence, and maybe I craved that. I'm not running my parents down, there was always food there, but we never had sit-down family meals and whatever my mum cooked, that was it, even at that stage in my life.

Our relationship quickly flourished, and it wasn't long before I was staying at her flat on a regular basis. At weekends I'd be leaving my clothes there, and slowly but surely things got more serious. I was very wary because of what had happened in the past, so I never permanently moved in there. I always made sure I went home to my parents' flat after a couple of days, but I used to stay there two or three times a week.

Despite my reservations, I enjoyed seeing Karen. She gave me a lot of affection, and I'd never experienced anything like that before. Maybe it was because I was shown a bit of love in a way my mother didn't. I'd had a hard, harsh upbringing. It's a very difficult thing to say, and I don't want to run my parents down, but the truth of the matter is, it was a miserable existence. I'd never had a lot of love in my home life.

It's nice when you meet someone and they look after you. You come home from work and you've got a bit of steak, egg and chips on the table, and your clothes ironed. I was thinking "Fuck, what's all this about? This is a new experience. I'm not used to this." With my family, no day was planned out. That just didn't happen. One day you'd go out and make £300. The next day you might not go out, because my dad's got the hump. Then there were the nightly rows, with his dinner going out the window. It was a very uneasy, unstable life. You couldn't plan anything.

Meeting Karen changed things. It gave me a sense of normality that I'd never experienced before. I could see myself staying with her long-term and building a family together. Whenever I was planning for the future, I included her in it. I never did that with Sharon, and I was too young to think like that with Julie.

We also shared another habit which was to affect every aspect of our lives. She might never buy it, but Karen would never turn down a line of coke. I wasn't any better, and that meant it started to play a prominent role in our lives. We were going out so much that we came to look forward to having a few lines. It was only on the odd occasion in the very early stages, but it was definitely there. I brought it in, and she liked it. Later on, I realised how much. By the age of 28, a year into our relationship, we were taking it every weekend. It was something that grabbed hold of us. That meant that as our relationship grew, so did our coke habit.

We used to spend a lot of time out in clubs up the West End in those days. I knew a couple of people I'd met through the scrap business at Stringfellow's strip club. I even met some of my dad's mates up there. That's where the coke started becoming more and more prevalent. I was going out most nights, spending a fortune. But it didn't matter, because all the while I kept on making more and more money. I thought it was never going to end.

The first time I realised that I was extremely wealthy was in 1991, when I was 29. I purchased my first Ferrari, a chiaro blue 328 GTS, off a city trader who was having money problems. It was an E-reg built in 1988 and would have been £150,000 brand new. He sold it through Lancaster's in Mile End for £43,500. I paid him cash on the day, no deposit. It was a nice car and I'd always dreamed of buying a Ferrari since I was a little boy. I'd already owned a Porshe, but a Ferrari is on a different level and it made me realise how far I'd come.

I'll never forget that as they drove it up the ramp out of the garage I had a tear in my eye. I didn't show it because I didn't want to let myself down. I got my bits of paperwork and all that stuff. In those days they'd tax the vehicle for you, so you'd show your cover note and go from there.

I remember I came out of that show room, which was opposite Bow Road train station, and turned left. As I drove away I had a tear in my eye. I was driving down Mile End Road and it was very emotional because I'd achieved something that was virtually unachievable for someone from my background. I'd actually got out of that poverty, and fulfilled my dream at a very young age. I'd done it without any education. I couldn't even read or write. I felt very strange about it. Even to this day I still do. No one helped me to do it. My old man educated me beyond belief. I would never tell him that, but it was priceless schooling, and a massive factor towards my success. The rest was my own hard work, pure determination, and knowing that I was never going to give in.

The first person I went to see after buying it was my mate Peter Brigg. I went to his house in Forest Gate. His jaw dropped when I pulled up. I did it because I didn't fucking like him, and I wanted to make a point. He was always running me down, and that fucking showed him. I was close to him, but we had rather a weird relationship. He was a bit insulting and a couple of times he nearly upset me, which wasn't a good idea in those days. He was a strange guy, and a stonemason by trade. He used to do a lot of work up the City, and earned a good living. When he knew I was a scrap dealer he used to take the piss out of me. But when I started cracking away with the shops I could see a bit of jealousy and bitterness creep in. They're saying "Well done", but they don't really mean it. They're just jealous, and would much rather see you with nothing.

Peter was a tight fucker who loved showing me his bank statement and boasting about having £30,000 in his account. I said to him, "Why don't you set up a couple of shops with that? I'll give you a couple of my contacts." It was a bad move on my behalf, since I'd been educated as a boy to not give your contacts away because people will end up treading on your toes, taking your business, and you'll learn a very costly lesson. No one gave me any contacts, I went and found them myself.

He didn't last long, anyway. He opened up two shops, one in Chingford and one in Brentwood. I helped him get them and he made money to start with, but he quickly gave up because his prices were too dear. After he'd opened them he pissed me off when he started going to my suppliers behind my back, and made a few sarcastic comments about me. I thought, "I'm cutting my own throat here." To turn him over I opened a couple of shops near his, and put my prices down so low he couldn't compete. It was his problem. I should never have given him a leg-up. I thought he was a good mate, but that was a bit of a misjudgement on my part.

After he went under, we made up and he ended up working for me. I had a massive 30,000sq ft warehouse in Witham by that point where I used to prepare and store all my furniture. It used to be a tax office, which is quite ironic judging by my later record. He ended up living there and was in charge of about 20 blokes I had working for me. He was quite happy to do that with his little bit of authority, which I was very grateful for. He lasted there around two years and then he fucked off. He went off in one of his moods, met some woman, and that was him hook, line and sinker.

He was never big into the coke, but he'd have a few lines. We used to go to a nightclub in Brentwood called Palms, which is now shut down. It used to perk him up because he was so miserable and moody. When he had a bit of powder up his nose he was a changed man and wasn't such a downbeat fucker. I was fucking thankful for that. But he didn't get involved in it too much. After he left my warehouse we lost contact. The last I heard of him he had a little warehouse selling urban military surplus stuff.

CHAPTER 7

—

COCAINE AND MONEY

The richer I got, the more accessible money I had. It wasn't tied up in property or offshore accounts like a lot of supposed millionaires. It was there in my hand, to spend when I liked. And believe me, I had no issue spending it. As I got really wealthy, people started to treat me differently. I don't know if they were jealous or they thought I knew something they didn't, but I noticed it. At the time, I didn't take too much notice of it and a few people took advantage of my generosity. They'd latch on for a free ride to feed their addictions. Most of these 'friends' came and went pretty quickly, as they have throughout my life. I wasn't too bothered, they weren't in short supply and I was more interested in getting out of my nut than building a deep meaningful friendship with someone. That's probably where I went wrong.

I should have known better, because my dad brought me up to believe that your friend is the new man who puts a pound note in your hand. It sounds a bit harsh, but at the end of the day it makes sense. A lot of people want to shit on you, run you down, sleep with your wife, get your business ideas, borrow money, and then fuck off and leave you with nothing. You're the best thing in the world when you're buying bottles of champagne and wraps of charlie for everyone. When that goes out the window, a lot of people desert you at a moment's notice. The richer I got the more I used to spend on people, which probably attracted the wrong sort. Not many people ever took me out for a meal. I was always paying the bill. It wasn't because I was a big-head or because I was flash, it's always because I've been a good-natured, generous man.

I would say that even though I became a junkie I remained a kind man throughout my life. I would always say to people when they came out, "It's going to cost money in here, I'll get it. Save your money and give it to your kids." I respect myself for that.

It rubs off from my father. Even though he was a rough and ready man, he was generous. That to me is gold dust which you can't buy. Certain people took advantage of that, the extent of which I didn't realise at the time. Looking back, they were taking me for a mug, but I was too coked out of it to realise what was happening.

Money kept coming in, fast and in large sums. It never calmed down, which in itself shocked me. I spent it just as fast as it came in. If I've got £10 I'll spend it, that's just the way I am. Now I know the cash may have come too quickly for me to channel it in the right direction. I spent it foolishly and wasted a lot of it. By 29 I had readily accessible money coming in on a daily basis, because I had shops all over the place. Even though wages, bills and rents were being paid, there was thousands of pounds in cash left over for me to spend on what I wanted.

As I expanded my business empire more and more, I devised a simple plan to make as much money as possible. It wasn't complicated and, like all good plans, it had a few clear messages. The first thing I would do was find shops with a very low rent, in secondary locations. I very rarely had a shop in the high street, they were normally in some back alley you'd be worried about getting mugged down. They might not have been pretty, but they were cheap. My average rent was £80 a week. I didn't have many shops that were more than £150 a week. The dearest shop I ever had was in Camden Town, by the lock in Eversholt Street, which was about £200 a week. I'd normally rent ones between £80 and £125 a week. I'd always go direct to the landlord with no agents creaming 20 per cent commission off the top. I'd get a six-month tenancy agreement, or just pay them every week. A lot were happy to do that when I turned up in my Ferrari and gave them the chat. I said they were going to get their rent, no issues. I said I had other shops to prove I wasn't bullshitting. Most landlords were quite happy with that. I'd put some money down and get the keys.

After that I'd advertise beyond belief, and be the cheapest by far. I'd start by letting everyone know until they were blue in the face that a pine shop was opening. There would be massive signs up in the windows. I'd put posters on lampposts. I'd have girls wearing tight tops handing out leaflets and giving all the kids free balloons with the shop's name on. Eventually I got paper baseballs caps made up with my branding on from a company in Braintree, Essex. Everyone would be talking about the pine shop. It would get to the stage that they'd be sick to death of hearing about this fucking pine shop. That was a common fact with my business. It might have been annoying, but mark my words, within two weeks of opening that shop would be heaving and making me a fortune. Often I'd say it was a closing down sale, just to get people interested. I did it so much that I even had the council coming round saying "You've got posters on lampposts advertising a pine furniture closing down sale and you've only been open a week."

My answer to that was "I'm just testing the water, but I did so well last week that I've managed to stay open another week." It wasn't illegal. Another trick I had was to put cars in lay-bys with A-board signs strapped to the roof which read 'furniture sale, closing down'. To reach out to more people I'd buy advertising space that hadn't sold, known as dead space, in local newspapers. If they went to press on a Friday I'd ring up on a Thursday and say, "What's the price?" They'd say £250 for the page. I'd say, "I'll give you £80 for it." Because they weren't going to get anything for it unless I bought it, they usually agreed. You could get away with it in those days. I did it so much that in the end they'd call me up all the time wanting to flog any dead space they had going. I was happy to oblige as long as I got it at a cut price.

I put this plan into practice just after I turned 30 when I opened a shop in Baker Street, Enfield, which I called Seconds Out. The rent was £80 a week. I spotted it when I was going past. It had a little sign in the window: 'To let'. I phoned it up and met the landlord, a rough and ready scaffolder who had a yard next door. His name was Mark and he was a big bald bloke who didn't mince his words. That's never bothered me, and we connected straightaway. I agreed to take it on the spot, so I gave him a deposit and a week's rent. He gave me the keys, so I got to work advertising it and moving stock in. Within six weeks of opening I was taking £6,000 a week.

I had another one in Chingford Mount that used to belong to a tyre company. It had a big loading bay at the back, and offices with a forecourt at the front. At the time, it was shut. I went up to the window and saw pound signs in my mind. I knew I could put canvas over the forecourt and furniture underneath. That would double my stock capacity for next to nothing. It was only £65 a week. I went in there and within a month I was taking up to £10,000 a week because my prices were so low.

It was basic stuff, but it worked and I went from strength to strength. To get everyone selling their best I was very strict with my staff. I'd pay them a basic wage and give them a massive commission. That meant that instead of customers going into a shop and having a gezza there not knowing what day it is, you get someone who's up and on their toes. It meant that if I was earning so were they. Some of my salesmen were taking home £800 a week in the early '90s – that was unheard of at other shops. Once bloke called Malcolm was getting around £1,000 a week. He was up, on the ball, all the time selling at the Chelmsford Shopping Village where I had two shops.

As well as advertising, I was also the cheapest shop by far. That really drew people in. I was nearly half the price of some of my competitors. If I bought a five-draw chest of draws for £85 I'd sell it for £140. Most shops would retail that for between £249 and £279. That means I'm at least £100 cheaper on one item. I sold over 400 different lines of furniture and I cut my prices to the bone on all of them.

My method was to buy solid pine furniture, no veneer, direct from the supplier. It was untreated and still had saw dust in the drawers. I'd get the boys at the warehouse I had working for me to give them a quick sanding and waxing. The finish wouldn't be perfect like it came out of Harrods but it was a rustic which was the fashion in those days. We used to do a run of one item, for example five drawer chests, and spend a day just prepping and waxing them. By the end of it I could have 30 ready. So do the maths. It cost me £15 to put it together, it cost £85 to buy and I sell it for £150. That's £50 profit. Multiply that by 30 that £1,500. That's just one line. I had 400 lines. I had everything from a bathroom cabinet to a King Charles Barley Twist bed. I bought the beds for £100, solid pine with a Victorian head and foot board. I'd wax them and sell them for £159. Most people were selling them for £300. I was nearly half price. People used to say, "but you only made £60 out of them." Other shopkeepers would say my prices were an "insult." My response was always "how many have you sold mate? I've sold 100 today. That's £5,000 profit." That's how I ran the business. I was never greedy and always cheap. Right down to the bone. No one could come in and honestly say they'd seen it elsewhere cheaper because it was impossible.

On the rare occasion that people did make that claim I'd go round and check. If by some miracle it was true I'd open up a shop nearer and I'd put them out of business by running at a loss. It was harsh but in business that's the way things are. If you can't handle it get a job.

Even though my profit margins were very low I could make it up in other ways. A lot of people who came in to get just one or two items ended up buying much more because I was so cheap. Work it out. If I'm making £60 from the bed, £50 from the chest of drawers and £20 from the bedside that is £130 profit in one deal. I'd regularly do 50 deals a day like that. Multiply that by 20 shops and it's big money. That's just a small deal. Imagine when someone comes in and buys a table and six chairs, kits out their kids' bedrooms, their bedroom and does their lounge.

Many times I'd do deals for up to £4,000. I didn't very often change the prices in the shops but I' do a package and say six chairs and a table, a barley twist dresser, an Ottoman, a toy box, two bedsides might be £499 one week. The next week it was £599. It got people interested and they were willing to spend more when they got a good deal. On an average £1,800 deal I'd make around £350. It doesn't sound like a lot but if you're doing three a day that's £1,000 in your pocket. As I got bigger I stopped doing so many deliveries and was essentially a cash and carry so I didn't have anything to do apart from hold my hand out and wave people on their way.

It was so successful that I ended up going into premises where previous furniture shops had gone out of business. One was in Epping Forrest. The landlord approached me and said they have gone under. I went in their quietly restructured it, resigned it and reopened. Within a couple of weeks, we're taking up to £10,000 a week. Not a problem. I was very on the ball, even though academically I couldn't read or write, I knew how to make a pound note. I was cheap and the product and service is good. People knew they're getting something they can't get anywhere else for that money. In the end, I didn't need to advertise because everyone was talking about the pine shops. "That bloke down there," they'd say. "How is he that cheap?"

In the end, I could compete with wholesalers on price. I had people coming to me who had pine shops up in other areas like Lowestoft, Norfolk. They'd buy it off me because I waxed it, so it was ready to go into their shop. It was cheaper from me than from a supplier. For instance, I'd sell a five- drawer chest for £159. They'd put it in their shop and sell it for £249 and still make £100 profit. That started to take off quite a bit, which highlighted how cheap I was. I even had some dealers coming in. I wasn't cutting my own throat, because if they were buying something off me for £150 and putting it in their shop for £250, they can't compete with me. There was nobody else around me who could compete. I don't think I could have done much more unless I started cutting down trees and making my own furniture.

The plan worked a treat, and made me a very rich man. I'd regularly go home on a Friday and Saturday night with £10,000 in my pocket. It worked so well that I'd get rival shops starting petitions trying to get me out. They'd say they put their life savings into their business, or their redundancy money from the sausage factory, and now I'm putting them out of business. My answer to that was "Tough. I'll buy your shop off you, how much do you want for it?" I did that many times.

With more money coming in, I was constantly increasing my stock by buying more lines of furniture. I got more contacts, and I wanted a bigger discount because I was buying on a bigger scale. I'm the first to admit I was hard to deal with, but I always paid. I had no credit. I was totally self-funded. I had two lorries, and I used to cram as much furniture as I could in them, just to meet demand. My philosophy was "stack it high and sell it cheap." People used to come and say, "When can you deliver it?" I'd say we don't, unless you're desperate. That was even from the little shops. I narrowed it down to doing very few deliveries. You'd get the odd occasional person who'd moan, but if you're saving £600 on a deal, what does it matter paying £35 to hire a van? Eventually I bought a couple of vans, and used to let the customers borrow them to take their stuff home. They were fully insured and it was all legal. Most people were happy with that, but you still got the occasional few who grumbled.

I never planned on staying anywhere too long, either. I basically got into a shop and absolutely caned the life out of it. If the takings started going down after a few months, I'd shut it and move elsewhere. Unlike a lot of businesses, I had no connection to one particular area. There was no attachment – I just wanted to make money. I was ruthless, and once things dried up I'd move on, no question. That meant I had a lot of shops, 30 over the years, but a lot of them weren't open for long periods. The successful ones, like the ones in Chelmsford and Baker Street, stayed open because they were profitable. But I had no emotional attachment to them. If they started making a loss I'd shut them straightaway.

By the early '90s credit and debit cards were really getting popular. A lot of businesses took them but I resisted and stayed as a cash-only business. People used to say "You don't take credit cards. Why?" I used to say, "I don't need to explain that to you mate, you're a customer." They'd say, "I don't carry cash" to which I'd reply, "Well I can't help you, have a good day." When I used to point out to people that they were saving £400 on a deal, most people changed their minds and paid. It was common sense. Being from the East End, I didn't like credit cards because I didn't trust banks. I like to have money in my hand where I can see it. It also means there's less of a trail letting everyone know how much you earn. The taxman gets a bit of money and they're grateful for what they get.

That's how I ran the business from the off. There was no complicated plan, and I don't think I ever actually wrote it down. It worked and went mental. I was making more money than I knew what to do with.

By my late 20s I eventually took the plunge and moved in with Karen. After my previous experiences living with women I was cautious, but things were getting serious and it was the next logical step. As it took off we quickly moved out of the flat in Queen's Road, Buckhurst Hill, and rented a few different houses. We flitted around a few places but never stayed anywhere too long. I liked to do a bit of a Lord Lucan sometimes, and would think nothing up upping sticks and moving house at short notice. During this time we became a family when our two boys, Martin and Albert, arrived in quick succession. Martin was born in Whipps Cross Hospital in 1992, followed by Albert two years later, after he was born at Finchingfield hospital in Braintree, Essex.

Strangely enough, having a young family didn't affect my outlook. I was happy to be a dad and loved spending time with my kids, but I was still driven by a desire to be someone. Something was lacking in my life and I still wasn't happy. Everything might have looked perfect with my business, money, partner and kids, but I still didn't feel happy. When Martin was very young I had a Ferrari Spider. There's a picture of Martin, in a Ferrari suit, and me in the Spider. In that picture I had a gold Rolex on and a pocket full of cash, but I still don't look that happy. I don't know if I ever will be.

I don't think being rich did it for me. I thought it would have made me happy, but it didn't. There's a scene at the end of *Only Fools and Horses* when Del Boy finally becomes a millionaire. He says, "I always wanted to be a millionaire, but now I am one it's not what I thought it was." That was how I found it.

I was supposed to have this perfect lifestyle, but it didn't satisfy me. For me it was more about the chase. I used to enjoy going out and finding things and selling things. Opening up shops and finding new suppliers and making money. I loved the adventure, and taking chances. All my life I've always been a chancer. Sometimes I got my fingers burnt, and other times it worked. When I finally got to that stage where I opened up the shops, the chase had finished. My inspiration was gone. I came to a crossroads in my life and instead of pushing forward the cocaine kicked in and I took the wrong turn. I couldn't see how it could get any bigger. I had the house, the partner with the fake tits, the kids, the money, the cars, but I think it got to a point where I thought: "It isn't as hard to achieve as I thought it would be, and now I'm here it isn't what I expected."

What I should have done is sat down and thought: "How can I take this to another level?" Maybe made the company a PLC and expanded into commercial markets. I didn't because I got complacent. I had money around me. It was coming in, and I got side-tracked with cocaine. When I got to the pinnacle of my success it wasn't what I thought it would be, and I felt unfulfilled.

As I chugged along, not knowing what to do with my life, we moved into a beautiful five-bedroom house in Great Dunmow, Essex. It had a massive double garage I could put my Ferraris in. I had so much money I paid for Karen to have a new pair of tits – the first of two sets. They were great to start with, but everything goes south in the end.

It was a posh area in Great Dunmow, and it showed by our neighbours. Mike Reid, the comedian and EastEnders actor, lived about 100 yards away. We cracked it off and he even bought about £2,000 of furniture off me. Another of our neighbours was a bloke from The Prodigy. He was all right, and I even let him have a go in my Ferrari. I ended up selling him £5,000 of furniture too.

The wealth just kept on coming and I couldn't spend it all, no matter how many cars or tit jobs I bought. I remember once when I went up into my en-suite changing room looking for a wrap of coke. Instead I found £8,000 in takings in my pocket. I didn't even know it was in there. It was nice, even though I had plenty of money back then.

I look in there now, and there's 8p.

CHAPTER 8

—

BUSINESS DOWNFALL AND INCREASING COKE

When the money really started to come in, my coke habit spiralled out of control. Very quickly it crept up from one gram at the weekend to £500 on a Friday night. I had a couple of blokes working for me who always had some to hand. I'd often have a few lines with them at work, before I bought some myself. Between 18 and my late 20s I did coke at a fair old whack. By most people's standards it would have been excessive. But I wasn't completely off my tits all the time. I had stages when it crept up and went down again. One week it might be £150. Then I might leave it alone for ten days before I spent £400 in a night on the stuff. I tried to fight it, but as soon as I had a drink I'd be back on the powder. As I lost myself with all the money, it crept up on me all of a sudden. My usage and the amount being spent on it were getting concerning, but I couldn't see it. I wasn't the fully-fledged coke-head I turned into, but I was out of control. It was becoming rife, and I was riddling my body with the dreaded powder.

In those days, I'd regularly have some coke before a meal, so I ended up just pushing my food around the plate. When I went home I often couldn't wait to order some powder in. It became a necessity. Like you need your car keys, I needed a bit of gear. Although the business was still functioning, and I wasn't a fully blown addict, I was on a dangerous road. I was in third gear, and before I knew it my intake had crept up to fifth gear.

Then it went from fifth gear to fucking turbo in the blink of an eye. That's why cocaine is so dangerous. You go from having £50 every fortnight as a little treat to let your hair down, to waking up and shoving six lines of coke up your nose at 8am, almost overnight. That's what happened to me, and it wasted 30 years of my life. I didn't know that then, it was only the early stages. I didn't realise how much trouble I was in.

You could be sat in on a Friday night, watching TV with your missus, when the cocaine man knocks on the door and your guard is down. You can't battle with it. You can try, but within 20 minutes you're going to go straight out to buy some. Then you're mingling with people on it, and it makes it very difficult to escape.

As my addiction went into overdrive, so did Steve's. We'd been friends since childhood, and he grew to love the powder even more than I did. Unlike me though, he didn't stop with cocaine. By his mid 30s he was a fully blown crackhead and was falling apart. I distanced myself from him: I didn't want him coming round my house when he was on the stuff, for obvious reasons. My kids were old enough to talk by this stage, and I didn't want them seeing him like that. He looked terrible and had lost all his self-respect. The drug made him dangerously unpredictable, too.

We went out one night and he tried to glass a woman in the face in a pub because she pissed him off. Luckily, she put her hand in the way so she was all right, but it just highlighted how unhinged he was. After that incident, I told him to fuck off and didn't want to see him again. He didn't listen and he came to the house in Great Dunmow one night totally wired on the stuff. Predictably we had a massive row which ended in a fight. It was very one-sided because he was totally fucked. I kept telling him there was no way he could win, but he didn't listen and continued coming at me. He finally gave up when he'd had a beating and couldn't stand. It was so bad I had to carry him inside to get cleaned up.

It was a horrific experience for us both, and I remember crying afterwards with regret. When he sobered up we made up and I said I'd help him get clean. He agreed, and when we parted I hoped that was the end of the crack. Sadly it wasn't, and despite promising to stay clean he went straight back on the stuff. A week later I got a call from his parents, who said he'd overdosed and died. His mother found him collapsed in his bedroom, with some crack-stained tin foil he'd been smoking it off. I couldn't believe it. He was my best mate, and he was dead.

We might have had our disagreements and he fell off the wagon, but he was like a brother to me. Steve's death should have been a wake-up call, and made me realise the danger of my own addiction. But like with so many warning signs in my life, I totally ignored it and went in the opposite direction.

After Steve died I tried to get over it by going back to running the business, which was really taking off. But the more money I took, the worse things got. By the age of 33 we were often taking £30,000 a week, and the business kept on growing. As we got bigger and bigger it started getting out of control. I was running an empire and I started to lose track of it. A lot of furniture was going through the warehouse to get sanded and waxed before being sold. It was getting quicker than I could manage. I was pulling up in the lorries, and it was actually sold before I could get it off. I had people waiting by the shutter in one warehouse for me to turn up. They were arguing over furniture, which is mental when you think about it.

I'm not an academic man by any measure, and I wasn't ready for it. I can count money and spend it, but the business needed to be structured more. I think if it had been I would have reaped the rewards even more. But, as a snotty-nosed kid from a rough part of East London, I didn't listen. Eventually I got an accountant, but before that Karen was doing the books. She wasn't a professional and was coked up a lot of the time, so they weren't done properly, or on time.

We started taking so much money that I got the taxman's attention. I had a visit from the VAT people in 1996 that left a big hole in my business. All my shops were in different names, sole trader this and that, so that raised a few eyebrows. They went through my books and made me pay about £40,000. The tax bill didn't put me under, but it did put the business under strain. The bigger issue was the fact that it too big for me to control. I was working seven days a week just to keep things from collapsing. I was getting fed up with it, and even though the money was coming in there was no time for myself. I had no social life. I was going out for a few meals here and there, but that was it.

As it got bigger, the logistical side of the business was out of control, and deliveries started to not turn up on time, or at all. I was having a few teething problems with staff, which I hadn't had before. Some of them weren't coming in, and everything was getting a little bit sloppy. The stress of everything not running smoothly meant I turned to coke even more. That's when my judgement started to go. My decisions weren't as sharp as when I first started, back when I had a tear in my eye from my first Ferrari.

I started taking things for granted. Instead of working I was swanning around in my Ferrari with a big Rolex on, thinking I was someone I wasn't. My relationship with Karen started to break down too. We were both doing a fair whack of coke on a regular basis, which didn't help things. Lots of money was being spent foolishly on things like watches, cars and clothes. On the odd occasion I was going out, I was spending extravagant money. It's quite sickening to think about now. I couldn't see it, but the business was slowly but surely coming to the end of its tether. Some shops started to take a little less money because I wasn't on point. I was a very easy man to work for when things were going well. But as they started to crumble it got more difficult.

The more gear I took the more irritable I got, which made me difficult to work with. I started mingling with people I shouldn't have been. Not Pablo Escobars, but undesirable characters. I was spending more time away from the business. Time indoors wasn't going too well. So things were getting a little bit sticky. I had more than £200,000 in various places, so I knew I could keep going. I never put money in a bank, that's not my style. My bank was a shoebox at my mum's house, or a wall cavity. I never liked banks, because you've got to ask them to take your own money out. Why would I go to a bank to keep my money safe? I had it where I had it, and if I wanted it I could get it.

As things fell apart I side-tracked myself by constantly changing my cars. While we were living in Great Dunmow I had a yellow Porsche 911RS N-plate and a Ferrari 328 GTS on a D plate to start with. I changed the yellow Porsche and bought a Turbo. Then I exchanged that for a Ferrari Testarossa. After a couple of months, I swapped that for a Spider. I took the Spider back and bought a 996. The list is endless. And it didn't stop with cars. I ended up with four Rolex watches that I didn't need. I bought top designer clothes for thousands of pounds a time, and only drank the most expensive wine and champagne. Then there were the endless tit jobs, botox and fillers that Karen had.

I started being a bit brash when I went out, too. Whenever I went anywhere with anyone I'd say, "Don't worry about that, I'll get that, put your money away." Being generous isn't a crime, and it doesn't make you a bad person. You might walk into a cafe and see two people with Rolex watches on asking for a glass of tap water. What's all that about? I'd be buying everyone in there a drink and ordering in a few wraps of coke. A lot of wealthy people are tight fuckers who never spend a penny they don't need to. That was never me. When I was wealthy I was cash-rich. If I wanted to raise £30,000 in a morning I could do it. No issue.

I wasn't one of these paper millionaires who's got all their money tied up in property but lives on their overdraft.

Wealth doesn't make you a bad person, but materialistic things are replaceable, whereas the things that really matter aren't. My mother, God rest her soul, said to me one day, "Son, money's for spending." That's why I was always spending. As I got richer I liked spending more and more. They always say people buy things they don't need because they've got a problem deep inside their mind. A psychiatrist once told me that. I didn't sit with her long because I thought she sounded madder than I was. But she was right. A lot of people buy things as an angle to escape.

Some people might go to a betting shop and put £50 on a horse. Some people might go out and meet a lady of the night. Maybe I bought luxury goods because I never had them as a child. But how many watches do you want to own? How many clothes and pairs of shoes do you really need? How many bottles of champagne do you want to drink? How much coke do you want to sniff? It was all a distraction from the fact that my business, and my life, were falling apart.

The money allowed me to stay in that bubble for a long time, without realising what was really going on. The wealth made me lose my way. As a man who'd been brought up with nothing, I should have known better. I lost my values and principles when I started making that sort of money. It makes you think you're something that you aren't. I was still a nice man, even though I was still under the curse of the white powder. I still helped people out if they needed any money for their rent. I always used to say "Give it back to me when you've got it. Don't tell me lies, and say you'll give it to me when you can't, because I'll get annoyed."

But coke, combined with the money, changed me. It made me a different person and altered my outlook. I was always a happy-go-lucky sort of person and a bit of a character. The money made me feel unstoppable and untouchable. Not like a gangster, because I'm not into all that and I know what goes down. But it made me lose the value of money and the knowledge of how hard it is to get. As a child I had a terrible and very unprivileged upbringing. Money didn't bring me what I thought it would. It brought me 80 per cent misery and sadness, which I wasn't expecting. The other 20 per cent was probably hidden by cocaine and drink.

With all addictions, things get to a point where you've had so much of it that you get bored. It might have taken me 30 years, but I eventually got to that point with cocaine. The stupid thing is that you'll keep using even after you're sick to death of it. I hope anyone who reads this will understand that.

You'll get sick death of your vice, but eventually it becomes a necessity. Like you have another coffee, you have another line, and another, and another. There's no buzz. You aren't going to get high. You aren't going to feel like the toughest man in the world. It's just going to take you deeper into yourself, so you have another line to bring yourself back from it. But it doesn't ever happen.

That is the tragedy of addiction. Addicts think that if they have another line it's going to bring them back. But they're wrong. It only takes you deeper into depression, deeper into that dark corner. My coke habit went from having it on an occasional night out in my late teens to habitually spending more than £1,000 on it every weekend. I started to make a point of buying it, whereas in the early days I wouldn't. Because the funds were available, a couple of hundred quid was one chest of drawers. Both me and Karen were constantly buzzing off our tits, using it socially a least twice a week. It was like "10am, a bit of grub, and bang, let's rock and roll on the gear."

The drink crept in just as fast as cocaine. I had the wealth around me so it passed me by, barely noticed. When you've got no money you notice any little cost. If a bottle of champagne is £10 and you've got £30 it's a big lump. If a bottle costs £400 and you've got £30,000, you don't notice the cost. As I started to drink more I got into good quality wine and champagne. I drank a lot of Smirnoff vodka too, in big tumbler glasses that I'd fill to the brim every morning. While living in Great Dunmow I joined a wine brokerage called Lay and Wheeler which was just down the road in Colchester, Essex. I'd spend thousands on boxes of Krug, Cristal and Dom Perignon Rosé. It got to a point where I was quite up to date with champagne and wine. I'd buy 12 boxes of six bottles of whatever I fancied. It was always on the understanding that I'd put a few away to let them age and sell them on. That never materialised because I drank them, and that was the end of that programme.

Spending a lot of time out of my nut, I came up with an idea. I realised that champagne and cocaine go together dangerously well. My money-making brain kicked in and I thought "I'll set up a company called Champagne Charlie." It would deliver champagne to all the coke-heads in the West End after midnight. There was nowhere in London which did it in those days, and it would probably have worked a treat. I got the leaflets and posters made up but it didn't ever materialise because a lot of my plans in those days fell apart when I put them off too long. You start off with all the right intentions at the beginning of the evening. You're sitting there thinking "What a great idea to make money." By the end of it you've had three bottles of champagne, three wraps of coke, you look like fucking Ken Dodd, and the plans never materialise. That's what happens with coke.

Slowly but surely, your decisions and judgement get very bad, and your life takes a downward slide. You can't see it, because the coke hides it from you. Eventually, when it does come back and hits you, you're fucked. You just can't believe how quickly it's all gone to shit. It's not easily repairable. You're at a point in your life where everyone's gone and you've only got yourself to blame. You've got to carry that guilt on your shoulders. Now you've got to try and get clean, which isn't easy.

The older I got, the more the relationship with Karen was on the rocks. She drank and took a lot of coke, and it was affecting her too. This was when we started drinking and taking a lot of coke indoors. We'd regularly stay in, get a few friends round, and take things from there. I'd get the drink out, throw the powder on the table and put some music on. To me that's a chequered flag, so the game's over, let the session begin. One of our regular guests was Karen's good friend, who loved coke so much we nicknamed her Dyson. She was the worst female coke user I've ever seen. She could stay up for days and keep on taking gear. Whereas other people would fade away, she got stronger and stronger. She could do four- and even five-day sessions with no issue. I know, because I used to sit there and do it with her.

I enjoyed a lot of those times, but it was a temporary fix hiding the real fact that we were falling apart. Anytime there's drink and drugs involved, the relationship is going to break down. Your mind goes, you get a bit agitated, a bit irritable, and you're going to clash. That makes an unpleasant atmosphere in the house. Sometimes you don't want them anywhere near you. You don't even want to look at them. From that point on you've got a problem.

Karen had a strong personality. She had to to be with me, and sometimes I didn't want that. I'm not a normal bloke. I don't suffer fools, and I'm not a fool. It got to a point where there were more and more rows. It was never violent, that's not in my nature, but it didn't make it a happy home and it was affecting the kids. We were arguing about everything from furniture not being done or delivered on time to who left the fridge door open. Coke gives you terrible mood swings. You fly off the handle in a split second. Someone leaving the TV on causes a full-blown argument. "Fuck the TV – I'll throw it out the window and get another one!" you scream. It gets to that point when you're on that wicket with someone, especially if you've got kids, and it's near-impossible to get off.

My parents weren't aware of what was going on. Most weekends I'd go and see them or they'd come and see me at the house, shops or warehouse. I had a very distant relationship with Julie at this time. When I got really wealthy my dad stopped doing scrap. I used to give him £400 a week, or whatever he needed to keep going. I used to look after the family as much as I could, that's the least I could do. I now wish I could have done more, but at the time I was drinking and taking coke. My mother was never aware of it. Even when she died, God rest her soul. Thank God she didn't. She had enough problems with my dad, who was still drinking. I don't hold it against him though, because I was a coke-head for 30 years. In those days, I didn't want them to know too much about me, so I'd do a Lord Lucan sometimes and disappear. My motto was "What people don't know they can't use to hurt you", even with family, which sounds harsh, but it's just how I am, and I still stick by that rule to this day.

CHAPTER 9

—

SPLITTING UP
WITH KAREN

Things continued to go badly at home, and everything was slipping because I kept taking coke. Eventually it got to a point where our relationship was effectively over. I can't just blame the gear. We'd been drifting apart for years. Things weren't great, even before the boys were born. It didn't help that I was working seven days a week and spending a lot of my time off my nut.

It sounds odd, but I think the money part of it didn't help either. So much money was about that we started bickering about stupid little things. She was moaning that we don't go out a lot and we don't do a lot. She would say "All we do is work, drink and do gear. Surely there's more to life." She had a point, but then she never refused a line of coke either.

I would put her up against most women who used to take cocaine. She wasn't in Dyson's league, but she wasn't far off either. She could stay up for two nights, no problem. I've done it with her many times over many years. She used to get a few of her friends round, very often Dyson, and we'd crack away. One thing led to another, and before you know it you're having a full-blown orgy. Cocaine sends your sexual desires into overdrive, and you do all sorts of things you wouldn't normally dream of. When you come round from it you feel dreadful, and realise you've done all these unspeakable things with people you barely know or like.

That started off as an occasional Friday night, but only got worse as the business progressed and I became a rich man.

No matter what happened at the weekends, the coke couldn't stop us drifting apart. We'd be all lovey-dovey for a few hours when we were out of our heads, but as soon as that wore off we started arguing. Our relationship was like being imprisoned, and we wanted to escape each other. We bickered about anything from money and the business to who'd left the TV on. We just weren't meant to be together. We were both strong personalities who clashed frequently. Cocaine made that a thousand times worse. The writing was really on the wall when she started to do a part-time beauty therapist course. She was doing nights studying at Ilford College. I thought: that's a big step forward from helping me manage a business turning over £30,000 a week. I told her that, and she wasn't too impressed. That ended in an argument – no surprises there.

Alarm bells really started ringing when she started getting in late. I knew something was going on but I didn't want to know. Even though we argued she was probably one of the first women that I loved, apart from my mother, and it was a real kick in the bollocks.

We were still living in Great Dunmow, Essex, when she said she wanted a break. Martin and Albert were about six and four respectively. Albert had alopecia when I left, and they said that was down to the break-up. That really pissed me off. Even though I was using the gear, I wasn't a bad person. It made me feel awful, and I was worried that Albert's condition was going to be permanent. Thankfully it was only temporary.

To add salt to my wounds, after we split up she ended up going off with one of my customers. He's a very well-known Lloyds Bank member called Freddie Young who worked in insurance. He owns half that fucking company. I had money, but he was something else. He was one of the main players in the insurance pay-out when the *Marchioness* boat went down on the Thames in 1989 and killed 51 people. That gives you an idea of how rich he was.

He was in his 50s then, so about 20 years older than Karen. I think he was a bit of a father figure to her. Either that or he was extremely well hung because she wasn't with him for his looks,

I can tell you that. The funny thing is, I had a blue Porsche 911 Turbo and so did he. It was exactly the same colour. Its reg was FY1, the flash wanker. He also had exactly the same gold Rolex Chronograph as me too, like he was trying to copy me. They hit it off when he came into my shop.

We were having a rough time, because I was using a lot. A lot more than what I should be, so you're slowly losing contact with each other. You're drifting apart, and obviously the rows crept in. After the split we were still in contact because we had two sons together, but it was strained. I was doing my own thing, floating around in my Ferrari and still making money.

Freddie had a mansion in Shenfield, Essex, and as an older man he was a shoulder to cry on. He wined and dined her and even took her skiing to San Lorenzo. But despite all his wealth, he was a coward. I had a bit of a run-in with him when I was supposed to pick my two sons up. Karen said "I'll meet you outside the Boar and Thistle pub in Buckerhurst Hill." When I got there he was sitting in the front of his car. I don't know what came over me, a bit of rage I think. I ran over to his vehicle and said, "Get out." He pissed himself in the car and refused to move. I don't like to be like that, even though I can be, because I'm not a bully-boy. After scaring him for five minutes I left, but after that he knew I wasn't a mug and he couldn't treat me like one.

Just weeks after our 'meeting' I learned that Freddie was still married. His wife rang me up and said, "Your girlfriend's going out with my husband, come and see me." I later went round to her lovely gated mansion in Ingatestone, Essex, with my mate John. When we got inside she offered me a drink and sat me down. She then went off to the kitchen to make a coffee, and came back in with a 12-bore shotgun.

She said: "Kill my husband and that bitch."

I didn't know if the gun was loaded. I didn't ask. It was a statement, that's for sure. She looked like Sybil Faulty with a bee's nest-type hairdo, and she had these mad fucking eyes. John said, "Fucking hell, the game's up, mate." I walked out there and thought "Fucking hell." Even as a man from East London, I thought that was a bit strong. The girl's come in with a shotgun to top her old man. At the time I was willing to take the money and do nothing. I thought it would be a nice bit of wages. She also had a white Golf convertible on the drive at the time. John said, "Can we take the car as a deposit?" She was up for it, but I thought better of it.

Afterwards I rang up Karen to tell her. She was with Freddie at the time. He said, "You've been round my wife's house", so we had another run-in. After I explained what happened, he said he was going to ring the police. The next thing I heard, she was sectioned. I don't think that's the first time she'd tried to top Freddie. Apparently, he had a bit of history for being a playboy and she didn't take it too well.

As soon as me and Karen broke up I started going out a lot to deal with it. I was partying more, trying to replace what I'd lost. That just caused my business to deteriorate even more. I still had excess funds, but I wasn't turning up for days at a time because I was shacked up round some bird's house getting high. I lost a bit of interest in the business because I had accessible cash around me. It was a fucking problem.

I was shutting down shops left, right and centre, and really cutting it back to the bone. I even got rid of the vans so people had to bring their own or rent one off someone else. I was basically just cash- and-carry at that point. In the end we even stopped waxing the furniture. I was buying white wood, untreated, and selling it on. I was still taking money, but my profit margin was so tight it was ridiculous. I shot myself in the foot because I put my prices down so low that when I went to put them up again it didn't work. I remember it very well. Takings went down very low. It was a kick in the bollocks, and instead of pushing on I just turned to coke even more.

I'd built up an empire very quickly, and earned a hell of a lot of money out of it. But money doesn't last forever, especially when you're going out and spending £1,000 a night on coke. I was spending a fortune on clothes as well. All those names which I thought were trendy. And being a generous man, I was always paying for everyone's coke. Having a few so-called 'friends' around me wasn't cheap either. They'd come round my house with £60 in their pockets, and I'd spent £1,000. It got to a stage where we partied so hard I started regularly calling out ladies of the night.

One night I called out a girl, spent nearly £2,000 and didn't even sleep with her. My friend was with me at the time. He remembers coming down in the morning and seeing me in my boxer shorts, coked out of my head with this stunning brunette Eastern European prostitute. She was sat there with the same clothes on and hadn't done anything apart from a lot of coke. I even got her to get me some. She came in and I said, "Do you want a couple of lines?" She got stuck in. Then I said: Can you get any more? She called her driver, who sorted some out and got a quarter for £250. I was still paying her £180 an hour. That happened many times. You're so out of it, you just want to talk.

When they go home and the gear finally runs out and you're completely drained, that's where the nightmare starts.

You're sitting alone in an empty house with nothing but your thoughts running through your mind. I used to think about my kids, my failed relationship and my dying business. It's not a nice place to be, and it only got worse.

I had a few brief relationships during this time. They came and went, if you know what I mean. Quite a few of them were nutty birds who were missing a few screws. A few were just complete headcases who should have been in an asylum. One even stalked me.

She was waiting outside my house in the middle of the night. Her name was Marie, and I met her in the Boar and Thistle in Buckhurst Hill. It used to be like The Sugar Hut back in the '90s. She was a nice-looking girl who loved a bit of powder. When I met her I was driving a blue Volvo estate because my Ferrari was being serviced. I got it for one of my sales reps because they're long and you can do a few deliveries in them. I told Marie, "I've got a Ferrari, you know." She said, "Of course you have, love." When she saw the Volvo she said, "I knew you were a bullshitter." I said, "Give me your number and I'll show you." About two weeks later, I went to see her at her house in Hertford Road, Cuffley. I turned up in my Ferrari, and when she came out her jaw dropped.

With Marie, we got on really well to start with. It was a rebound thing, after I'd been with Karen for a long time. I used to take my boys round there. She used to work for Ford on the reception, and drove an XR3 convertible. To start with it was fun, but very quickly she started getting possessive because I was getting through the break-up so I was up and down. I dealt with it by getting on the gear. She was on it too, which only made matters worse.

I remember one night I took her to Stringfellow's. My doorman friend let us straight in. It was when the Page Three model and Sam Fox lookalike Maria Whittaker was celebrating her birthday. Terry Marsh, the boxing promoter who got shot, was also there. You couldn't get in there, but with my friend on the door we got straight in there. Within five minutes I was speaking to a fella with long hair called Marilyn. It turned out he was one of Boy George's exes. As we're talking, Marie is tapping me on the shoulder saying, "Have you got any gear?" She's going to the toilet and coming back 10 minutes later off her tits.

Later on that night I met a little fella in his 60s called Curley King who was surrounded by models. He was very well known in the East End and after we got talking it turned out he knew my dad. He told me a few stories about things that happened back in his day. It was quite emotional for me, because I rarely talked about my dad. Usually I associated him with getting grief, so it was nice to hear some funny anecdotes about his antics in his youth.

Curly King was a very good friend of Peter Stringfellow. Peter was there that night, but I didn't say anything to him. I ended up coming out at 6am, completely off my head, with Marie. We went to a hotel and were getting down to the nitty-gritty when she realised she'd forgot where she parked her car. She was that out of it on coke she couldn't remember. She started panicking, and went into one. That was the end of that night of lust. It's just an example of how coke can ruin your evening.

When Marie started to get very possessive I said I wanted to slow things down. She didn't take it well, and started stalking me. I was in a restaurant in Crouch End right by one of my shops when she walked in, screaming. She tried to glass me, so I put my hand up and the glass broke across my thumb. I've still got a scar on my right hand. After that she basically lost the plot. Her mother started to ring me. She started going into one of my shops in Baker

Street, Enfield, and asking where I was. When they wouldn't say, she caused scenes. I'd ended things, but she kept contacting me. The final straw came when she said she was pregnant and tried to get £800 off me to pay for an abortion. I knew it wasn't true, and I approached her mother. She went mental. Her mother said there's something wrong with her. That had a very sad ending. She wasn't a bad girl, but she had a screw loose.

Shortly after that ended I met a wealthy Jewish girl called Wendy. She was about 6ft tall with dark hair and a slim figure. She wasn't just a pretty face though, and was very switched on business-wise. She was one of the first people in the country to get a franchise for The Tanning Shops. She had one in Barkingside, and made a lot of money out of it. She liked good music, good food, and had a bit of style, so we clicked. We used to go to a few clubs in the West End like Hanover Green and Heaven, the gay club. She didn't do gear, though. I remember she used to say to me, "I don't know why you do that stuff. You change into a different person."

Her father was a very wealthy man. He owned all the hotdog stands in Wembley Stadium for around 30 years. Her mother was a traditional Jewish woman who hated me from the off, even though we got on well together. She once said to me "Martin, there's no way you're going to stay with my daughter. I know what you're about. I've got you down to a T."

Soon after we got together she started to get very jealous. I was always driving around in my car, thinking I was something I wasn't. I had accessible cash and I was always out, off my head. A lot of her friends were saying "I've seen Martin out with another girl." I was going through a rough patch with women. I just wanted a bit of love.

When you're on the coke you tend to hurt a little bit. When she heard about the other women she started to get very possessive. She used to follow me about in her BMW convertible 3 series. Any clubs that I went into, she'd turn up. It was embarrassing. I think she was looking for a full-time relationship, but I was using the gear and she wasn't. You can't connect if they're not on the gear and you are, because you're on a different fucking level. You're 6,000mph turbo and they're still in neutral. Your cravings and your desires are extreme, and they just can't compete.

It came to a sad end after six months. I was in a Travelodge in Eastern Avenue. I'd been up for two days on the gear. She rang me and I said I was there. She put a letter under the door which said, "I can't see you any more." I was expecting a bit of how's your father, so it was a shock when I realised it was over. I was relieved in a way, because being followed around was creepy.

The next mental girlfriend I had was an Irish woman called Marie. She was a slightly chubby but pretty girl with blue eyes and dark hair. She worked in an office and was desperate to go back to Ireland after splitting up with her long-term boyfriend. We were together for an eventful three weeks. We met when she came into the Enfield shop to buy some furniture. It was only small but used to take a lot of money, sometimes £10,000 a week, so I'd often hover around there giving customers the chat. She came in, and even though she was a bit older than me and dressed like a granny we hit it off. I took her out for a drink in a place called the Townhouse in Enfield. I offered her some coke, which turned out to be a very big mistake. She had a couple of lines and took a turn for the worse.

When we got back to her flat she went mad and started freaking out. She was looking out of the window thinking someone was there. I was laughing my bollocks off. I told her there was no one out there and got her to sit down. We were drinking Jacob's Creek wine and I said, "This stuff sends you up the creek." She didn't find that amusing. I met her a couple of times after that. On one date I took her to the Broadway in Muswell Hill in my Ferrari, which she loved.

On our last date she said she was going back to Ireland to live with her parents. She asked me to go with her. For some reason I agreed, even though I didn't really want to. She went off and arranged everything. I bottled it a few days before we were going to leave. I thought "I can't, she's got a screw loose." Rather than tell her the truth, I did a Lord Lucan and went on the missing list. Instead of taking the hint, she came after me like some sort of fucking assassin.

She came in the Enfield shop shouting and screaming: "Where is he?" The sales rep at the time was a very good friend of mine. An Irishman and a character himself, he said he had to fight her off. Later on she rang me up because she'd given me a portable TV with a video player. I think I threw it out of the window. She wanted it back. I told her she could have a new one, and left it in the shop. I stayed well clear of that shop when she came to pick it up. I didn't want a knife in the back. Thankfully she didn't cause any more dramas and I never saw her again.

I thought my luck might change with my next girlfriend. I couldn't have been more wrong.

Paula was a stunning blonde in her mid 20s who had a fantastic figure. She was also one of the heaviest female users of coke I have ever seen. Karen was in League One, this woman was Premier League, second only to Dyson. Like so many women in my life, I met her in the Boar and Thistle pub. She was a well-spoken West

End girl who worked in promotions for Fortnum and Mason's, so she had all the chat. She came over and we started talking. At that time, there was a club called Charlie Chan's at Walthamstow dog track. After we got past the pleasantries I took her there and we connected straightaway. We were both using a lot of gear, which I thought at the time was good, but it meant the amount of coke we were taking went through the roof. We'd regularly sit up and do £600 of gear between the two of us. She could do two grams in two lines. One nostril, one line. I thought, "That used to be my trick." She lived on the Great Cambridge Road on the A10, and I'd go round there regularly and have three-day benders.

Over the next five months we had a very erratic, lust-filled relationship. It really did get hot. When you're using cocaine your sexual drive can go through the roof. Sometimes you want to do things that you don't know exist. She thought it was fantastic at the time. We were having a great sexual relationship that was never going to last. She was addicted to gear, maybe not as bad as me, but maybe worse. She used to ring me up at 4am, completely wired, and want to come round.

It was a whirlwind that fizzled out. She was too much, even for me. If you said "Let's do gear seven days a week", she would. She could stand her ground with anyone. It got out of control, and she was ringing me up insisting that I ordered more. I was flush for money so it wasn't a problem, but in the end it just wore itself out. Sexually we went to the limit. We were both off our tits, so there was never going to be a relationship. Eventually she ran up a £400 bill with a friend of mine who I was buying gear off. He rang me up and was pestering me for the money, so she was causing me problems. I ended it at that point but she couldn't let go and started turning up at my shops with her mate, causing scenes.

She eventually took the hint and moved to Marbella in Spain. She hadn't learned her lesson from buying drugs on tick in the UK, and was soon in debt with a drug dealer for about £1,500. She got worried because he was a bit of an unsavoury character to say the least, so she cleared off. A few weeks after she left for Spain I got a call in the middle of the night. She was in Puerto Banus with some bloke. She said, "Someone wants to speak to you." He said, "Paula's been talking about you. You're a nice man." They were both fucked, and waffling on. Eventually the phone ran out and I never bothered ringing them back.

I thought that was the end of it but a couple of months later one of my mates, another heavy user, called me up. He lived in Hainualt, Essex, and said, "Do you want to come round? I've got two birds here." Before he'd put the phone down I was gone. When I got there Paula was sitting there coked out of her head, in just her knickers and a bra, with another woman. It was about 8.30am, so they'd been up all night. It was a sad experience, because she broke down and wanted a cuddle. My friend ended up going off with her friend, and I got a cab home.

It sticks in my mind to this day. She was all coked-up, and had come to the end of her tether. You need a bit of help, but how are you going to get help off people who use coke? All they're going to do is offer you another line. They'll say, "Don't drive yourself mad, have another line." What kind of help is that for an addict? That's the last I ever saw of her, but I'd be very surprised if she didn't have a very bad ending.

I carried on having one-night stands, most of them with fellow coke users. I think that's why lots of them came back with me. In my experience, if you throw a bag of powder on the table it goes from there. But it wasn't fulfilling. I was burying my head in the sand, spending days coked-up with women I barely knew. All the while my kids were growing up and my business was falling apart. It all weighed heavily on my mind. Things got to a point where I decided something had to change.

CHAPTER 10

—

GOING TO AMERICA

Right from being a little kid I'd always dreamed about going to America. In the UK people used to say, "They'll love you in America because you're wild, outrageous and outspoken." It turned out they were right. Before I set off I toyed with the idea of going to Thailand but then I thought "Fuck it" and booked a flight to Miami. It was about four months after I split from Karen, and a spur-of-the-moment decision. I took about £30,000 in cash with me, so they stopped me at the airport and held me for 14 hours. The laws are different over there, and they probably thought I was a drug dealer. I remember I had this big black female American passport control officer who took a liking to me. She said, "I'm going to get you through. Say you're investing in a condo. I'll get you another flight from here to West Palm Beach. Then head to a place called Boca Raton in Florida."

I followed her instructions and arrived there the next day. It was a very wealthy area full of unbelievably attractive women. In the terminal building there's a great big board with all the hotels' names on it. I pressed the button for my hotel, the Holiday Inn, and a limo came and picked me up. I remember thinking, "This is the life."

On my first night, I went to the Martini Bar in Boca Raton. Within ten minutes of being in there I spoke to the doorman and he said, "Oh Jeez, I like your accent." I said, "Can I score a bit of gear?" He offered me an 'eight ball', which is called an eighth, or 3.5g, in the UK. It cost $150 so was a lot cheaper than the UK, where it would be well over £200. As well as being cheaper, the gear was much purer, because it's much closer to the source. Within a day of being there I was getting it as regular as clockwork.

I was getting through about two 'eight balls' a day, which was overboard, but because it was cleaner you didn't get so much of a comedown. When you use cocaine that's cut with a lot of stuff you get blocked sinuses. In the US, it was very clean so you get a massive rush very quickly, but it doesn't last very long. Some coke is called creeper because it gives you a slower rush, but then the comedown is horrible. It wasn't like that in America, which might sound like a good thing, but it isn't because it just means you take more.

With a steady supply of coke whenever I wanted it I cracked on. It was fantastic, and I thought I was in heaven. The beach was beautiful. The women were stunning. The food was great. Everyone was so friendly too. You've only got a buy a newspaper and people are like "Wow, you're a lovely guy." For the first four weeks I was having the time of my life.

I struggle to remember most of it. I used to go to a place called the Sportif Bar, completely out of my nut. They loved me in there, and all the waitresses called me 'the fella from East London'. I was in there one day, off my head, when a waitress said, "You've got a phone call." I was paranoid, thinking the FBI was after me because I hadn't bought that condo. She gave me the phone and a voice at the other end said, "Hello, my name's Terry, I'm the owner of the bar. Can I buy you a drink?" I looked down the end of the bar and she was there on the phone. She was a stunning six-foot-two ex-model in her mid 30s with a figure to die for. From there on in we had a very passionate relationship. On the first night, she took me to another place called Martini Tow Bar, before we went straight back to her place. It was a beautiful house on the river with its own speedboat. Her dad was a very wealthy congressman called Ted. He had an old Corvette and a Stingray which he let me drive, much to my delight. Terry liked using coke just as much as me, so we had some common ground. We took so much I can't remember much of our first night. The next morning, I woke up in her water bed with a raving hangover, thinking I'd dreamed it all.

I quickly established a routine of lounging around in the daytime, turning red as a lobster, and spending my evening getting out of my nut in Boca Raton's numerous bars. Most days I'd get up around midday and head to a breakfast bar called Denny's. I'd sit there all day, popping to the toilet every 30 minutes to have a line, all the while making people laugh. Then in the evenings I'd head out to a bar, score some more gear, push my food around the plate, and party the night away.

One evening, when Terry was away, I went for a meal in a place called the Asta Bar. It was a two- second walk from where Gianni Versace got shot. I was out of it so I was just pushing food around my plate, when I got talking to this unbelievably beautiful blonde woman who looked like Pamela Anderson. She invited me back to her house with her husband – a wealthy Irish-American. They had a lovely house right on the beach. We got bang on the gear until the early hours, which sent our sexual desires into overdrive. I ended up going to bed with the pair of them. From what I can remember it was quite an experience.

I woke up at 11am the next day with a terrible hangover. I thought she was lying beside me with her arm hanging over me. When I looked up I saw it was her husband. I got out of that bed faster than Linford Christie, and never saw either of them again.

After a few weeks in the Holiday Inn Terry suggested we went to Miami. She knew people up in the film industry there, and got me a cheap hotel room. I happily agreed and we headed there. The partying was even worse in Miami, and the coke was even purer. Every night we'd be out on the gear and living it up. Between the brief moments of fun, I began realising that I wasn't happy there, and was just running away from what really mattered. My relationship with Terry was also coming to an end. The more I got to know her, the more I realised she was slightly mental. She had a death wish and always used to drink and drive, even when she was completely smashed. We were both living a lie, and the coke and drink couldn't hide that. We weren't 20-year-olds who had no commitments. She had two daughters and I had my two boys, who I missed more every day. As the realisation that it wouldn't last forever kicked in, the passion drained out of our relationship.

I began to question what I was doing there. When I told Terry I was thinking about leaving, she was desperate for me to stay, and suggested we get married. I flirted with the idea, but after four months I knew I'd worn it out. I missed my sons, and whenever I spoke to them they were saying "Come home, we miss you. We don't like it because Freddie's round here." He told them to hold a book under each arm when they ate dinner so they did it properly. He used to insult me too and say, "Your dad doesn't know what he's doing." It was hurtful knowing my kids were round there, living under his roof. He might have been a high-flying businessman, but I thought he was still a fucking mug. That made me question even more what the fuck was I doing there out with all the Yanks.

I was just trying to get away from the truth. I was running away from my partner and kids, living the life of Riley. It just came to an abrupt end, and I decided to head home. I'd had enough of doing gear all day and making strangers laugh.

My six-month tourist visa had nearly run out when I arrived back at Heathrow. I had £1,200 in my pocket from the £30,000 I'd taken with me. It's funny because the moment I got back I wished

I'd never left. When I got on the plane from America the sun was shining and everyone was happy. When I arrived in England it was raining and everyone had long grey faces. I came back to doom and gloom but I suppose that suited how I was feeling inside.

I loved spending time with my sons, but my problems didn't disappear when I got home. I was still unhappy about the break-up, not having my kids living with me, and the fact I was no longer this high-flying businessman. Before I left I'd sold six of my shops to my accountant. I'd kept three shops on. The ones in Chelmsford, Romford and Chingford were being run by my salesman Malcolm, with my dad collecting the money, while I was away. He did his best and they were still making money, but it wasn't like before. I'd lost my spark and enthusiasm for it.

Maybe deep down I realised that I wasn't happy when I had dozens of shops and turned over £30,000 a week, so why would I be happy if it went back to that. My lack of desire meant the business was all over the place, so I cut it down to two shops. In the end I got sick of it and sold them both off for £15,000.

When I eventually packed up, the people who worked for me cried. They said to me, "Martin I've never worked for a man like you in my life. You're an easy-going fella. We love you. You're a character." It was an emotional moment for me, because I had some good loyal people there. But by that stage the cocaine had started to take its toll, and I couldn't function like before. I was on a very self-destructive road to rock-bottom. I couldn't be arsed with it. I'd lost a bit of drive, and started mingling with people I shouldn't have been. I'd been swept away in a sea of addiction and misery.

It was a very difficult time in my head, and I got through it with the help of cocaine. I drowned my sorrows with the drug.

It was a temporary fix, and I was losing myself to the powder more and more. The problems disappear when you have a line, but when they come back they're a hundred times worse.

My usage only got worse because money wasn't an issue. I had about £150,000 stashed away so I could do what I wanted. As well as going out I distracted myself by buying luxury items like Rolex watches and designer clothes. When you're going out and spending like Bill Gates, even £150,000 doesn't last long. I couldn't see that then, and with loads of so-called 'friends' around me who took coke I just became more and more hooked on the powder.

CHAPTER 11

—

BACK WITH KAREN

E ngland's doom and gloom didn't do my coke habit any
favours. To get over the breakdown of my relationship and
closure of my business I spent most of the time out of my nut.
Heavy nights up the West End were a regular occurrence, and I
lost count of the number of three-day benders I had. No matter
how good the night was, it always finished with sadness. It would
end with me alone in a hotel room unable to sleep, with only my
thoughts for company.

I couldn't escape the darkness in my head, and it really
affected me. The most upsetting thing was the fact that my kids
were growing up without me. I've never liked broken homes.
My mum and dad went through their highs and lows but
they stuck together through thick and thin because they're
old-school. I felt a failure because I never managed that, and
dwelled on it constantly. Throughout this time I was still in
contact with Karen because of the kids. Every time we spoke I
used to wonder whether we could get back together. I thought
it might not be too late to save the relationship and start all
over again.

With this swirling around in my head I phoned her one
night, completely out of my nut. That's what you do on cocaine.
You make random phone calls to people. I got so lonely that
sometimes I'd ring up pizza people just for a chat. Freddie
answered and put Karen on. When she asked where I was I
started having a panic attack. I was outside Chingford Station,
and I collapsed. I still don't know if it was an overdose or a panic
attack. Maybe it was a bit of both. An ambulance came and the
paramedics gave me glucose to wake me up. I still wasn't well
so Karen came to pick me up and took me back to her flat, where
I passed out on the floor. I woke up a day later with a terrible

hangover to find Freddie standing over me. He said something about getting me out of there because I was really ill. Normally I would have argued back but I was in such a bad place I couldn't even muster the strength to call him a wanker. My head was all over the place, and the coke and drink just made things worse. I ended up leaving later that afternoon and going home, where I collapsed. For some reason that experience made me focus more on getting back with Karen. I thought it was the only way to fix things and find happiness.

It wasn't long before I got my chance to rekindle our relationship.

I was in Epping Forest Country Club one night when she walked in, made up like a dolly bird, showing off her fake tits. I couldn't resist, and we had a night of incredible lust. After that we pretty much kicked off were we'd ended two years earlier. She left Freddie's flat in Shenfield and we moved back in together. A friend of mine had sorted me out with a small flat in South Woodford, Essex. It was a bit of a shithole but I didn't care, I had my family back. Having the boys about and living with Karen made me feel better about life. The logical next step was to get married. I can't even remember proposing, I was that coked out of it, but she must have said yes.

With no business to run, I was using gear seven days a week. Even when I didn't go out I'd get on the powder. I was trying to delude myself that I'd found happiness. On the face of it I had, but I still have a very stormy relationship with Karen and we should have never got back together. My parents weren't too thrilled about the wedding, my mother especially. My mum refused to come, and my dad just turned up briefly at the registry office before he fucked off.

The night before the wedding, we got on the gear and were up until 4am. We nearly cancelled the service because we felt so rough. I was tempted, but then I thought getting married was going to be the beginning of my new happy life so I dragged myself out of bed at the last minute. We had a brief service at the registry office and then headed off to the Le Pont de La Tour restaurant near Tower Bridge. There were only four of us at the reception, including Karen and myself. Our only other guests consisted of my best man, a character called Mark, and his then girlfriend Sue. We'd got on the coke before we got married, so by the time we sat down for the meal we were so out of it that we couldn't eat anything. I wanted to make a speech, but the head waiter came over and told us we couldn't do that. Mark went off into the toilet with him and gave him a bit of gear. The bloke came out all over the place and said "Crack on."

I can't remember much of what I said, and I'm not Laurence Olivier, but it seemed to make people in the restaurant laugh. After that I ordered a bottle of 1963 Krug champagne. It costs £750 a bottle and was 35 years old when we got married in 1998. Everyone was watching the waiter open the bottle, hoping he'd spill some. He didn't, and it went nicely with all the powder. Because we were all so fucked on the gear I bought everyone in the bar, about a hundred people, a drink. We ordered more bottles of champagne, and when I went to pay the bar bill came to £5,500. That was without food. I spent all my money in there so on the way home I had to pay the cab driver with a wrap of coke. He was more than grateful for that.

I took two days to recover from that session. I got so fucked that I couldn't remember where I'd parked my dragon green BMW 640 coupe. I spent days wracking my brains until

I finally remembered that I'd left it in an NCP car park next to Tower Bridge.

A few weeks after the wedding I had a function at a place called Manor Hall in Chigwell, Essex. I rented the hall out for about £5,000 and had a big party. Both our parents agreed to come this time and I had a few of my skulldugger mates round. We got on the drink, but it was more of a family affair so wasn't too messy. Normally at an event like that I would have gone turbo, but I've always respected my mother and I didn't want to her to see me like that. So I calmed it down about twenty levels, which meant it wasn't the most memorable night. It should have been a happy occasion, but because I wasn't coked up I was just miserable.

It's sad, but that's what the drug does to you.

As we settled into married life I decided we needed to move away from London to be happy. I carried on this habit for many years, and it was never successful. I still have over £200,000 in cash stashed away in various places. The only issue I had was to find somewhere to start our next adventure.

CHAPTER 12

—

WEST MERSEA

Our next adventure would be in West Mersea, a picturesque seaside island in Essex that's within spitting distance of the beach. I came across it by chance and found a beautiful six-bedroom house about 30 seconds from the sea. For £1,400 a month it also came with a huge garden, a double garage and a drive that could easily fit 10 cars on.

When we moved there I thought it was the start of something new. It was the beginning of a new life away from arguments, coke and booze. That wasn't the case as your problems follow you, no matter where you go.

Within a few days of getting there I saw a massive warehouse for rent. It was an old chandlery for boats that was sitting empty. Light bulbs lit up in my head and I immediately thought I could turn it into an auction room. I went to see the landlord – a proper old fisherman who smelt like he hadn't had a bath in a year. He said he had another yard down on the sea front, so didn't need the second one. Despite the smell we got on all right, and he agreed to rent it to me for £200 a week. I was going to call it Treasure Island, and I even got signs and portholes made up. It had an office at the front and I imagined that people would come in there with their paperwork before heading to the warehouse round the back. I spent fortunes advertising it and telling everyone it would be opening soon. That never happened, for reasons I will explain shortly.

With all my excess cash I didn't need to work to stay afloat. I needed a distraction to give me something to do. With the auction house never materialising, I started selling cars. When we left London, I got rid of my Ferraris and Porsches and had Mercedes instead. We had two 500 SLs, a coupe and a 2.8 litre silver Audi convertible with a blue roof. I bought a couple of them at an auction and that got me thinking that maybe it could be a little money-earner. After that I started regularly buying cars at auction, getting them professionally valeted and selling them on. I used to use a firm called Smart Brothers and Auto Glean who made them sparkle before I advertised them in shop windows. It was quite successful and I used to sell a lot of Mercedes estates. I'd buy them for £1,500, valet them and make them presentable before flogging them on for £3,500. It wasn't illegal, but one trick I used to employ was to change the log books to female owners because people think that's more genuine. I used to get called all the time. Some weeks I was doing £4,000, and it was all cash.

All the while I was selling cars I dreamed of opening the auction house. I wanted to get back to earning the sort of money I had with the pine shops. It was possible, but the gear and booze were holding me back. From the moment I moved to West Mersea I was bang on both of them. That place was one of the worst times on the gear in my life. I was doing about £1,000 of coke a week, and probably drinking twice that in champagne. I was drinking every day, and starting to develop a real problem. Even though we'd just got back together I wasn't getting on with Karen, which just made things worse.

My lifestyle was out of control. I was avoiding reality, constantly sitting there laughing and joking with people I barely knew, totally coked out of it. Everyone you met down there was on the gear, which didn't help my addiction.

I got friendly with a couple called Keith and Linda. He had big ears like Ken Dodd, and an IQ that would rival a six-year-old. I remember we went out for my birthday one year. We were drinking and got a limo to take us for a Chinese at a place called Wong in Witham. Both me and Karen got bang on the gear the minute we got there. I kept it a little bit sly and didn't tell them while we were in the restaurant because I didn't know how they'd react. But when we got back to his house, which had its own swimming pool, I said, "Do you want a bit?" As I said it I turned around and saw a picture hanging on the wall of his dad on a police horse. It turned out he was the police commissioner for Stoke Newington.

I literally shat myself and just froze. He saw me looking at the picture and then the gear. We looked at each other but he said, "Don't worry. I'm not going to say anything." But I thought "Bollocks!" and went paranoid for the rest of the night. I wanted to get the fuck out of there as soon as possible. Eventually me and Karen got a taxi. I couldn't wait to get home. I'd had a bad turn and just wanted to be alone. He didn't say anything, and why would he? Having a bit of coke is hardly crime of the century.

But the drug makes you paranoid. You think MI5 are going to smash down your door for two grams of gear. You know that's nonsense and you tell yourself not to worry, but it's no use. You're trapped in that thought process and it's almost impossible to break out of it. After that night we stayed in contact and they later helped me out, but I made sure they never saw me to do coke again.

All through that time things were right in my mind. I'd lost my desire to do anything. Deep down I knew it, but I was in denial. If you hit coke hard enough your problems don't exist, so that's what I did. I had lots of money around me, which made it easier for my addiction to flourish. If someone bought a car and I was in bed I'd say, "All right, come round." I'd drag myself out of bed, make the sale, and then go back to getting smashed. I was still making money, which isn't a crime, but it made it easy to keep taking drugs. I think boredom came into it too. I was doing nothing with my life.

The relationship was on its arse. The partying was getting out of control. I was moving around trying to escape my problems, when I should have confronted them. Moving never solves your issues. You say "We'll move and start afresh." Bollocks! I could go out now and get gear in 30 minutes. If you know how to talk to people you can get some coke anywhere.

I had some terrible times in that house. It wasn't just coke, I hit the booze just as hard. I drank a lot of champagne there. Lay and Wheeler, wine merchants, was only four miles away in Colchester. I even had an account there, and used to buy cases of Krug, Crystal and Dom Perignon every week. The more I took, the more fed-up and depressed I felt. I had mood swings, and was getting down a lot. That's probably why the auction house never took off.

I'd put off opening it all the time. In the end Karen used to do the ironing in the chandlery, and I used to sit in there and drink bottles of wine. It was like a social club. People would come round and get smashed with me. I'd always say, "We're opening next week, don't worry." It never happened, which is a shame because it could have been a good business. As well as making me miserable the booze, my poor diet and lack of exercise made me put on a lot of weight. I'd always been a slim guy growing up, but in West Mersea I ballooned up to about 17 stone.

As I became more and more trapped in my own drug-fuelled world I had a mad idea. I thought I could kick the auction house off by holding a huge motorcycle auction one weekend at the warehouse. I even put an ad in *Autotrader* telling everyone that there'd be this giant sale. I arranged it and loads of people turned up one Saturday morning with their bikes.

Unfortunately, the night before the sale I had a massive session on the gear.

I was still in bed at 9am when my phone started ringing constantly. I had the geezer who owned the unit ringing me saying, "There are thousands of bikers outside waiting to get in." I went "Bollocks to them", and I never opened up. I had Hell's Angels round there going mad, and I was still in bed. They even came round to my house and started throwing stones at the window. They were shouting "Are you in?" I was out of my nut crawling across the floor so they couldn't see me. It wasn't just the gear, me and Karen'd had a row about something stupid, and things got heated. When you're on gear your mood can turn on nothing. It was very up and down. When you have a bit of gear your heartbeat gets up and your mind wanders into places that you don't even think about. It escalates. You might owe £10 for your phone bill, and by the end of the night you're ready to jump out of the window. That's how I was that day. I was so bad I just couldn't face seeing people, even though I'd have probably made quite a lot of money out of that auction.

But I'd got to such a low at that house that I couldn't face it. The experiences I had there were terrible. I wasted a lot of money there, more than £150,000 in about a year. I was buying things for the sake of it. I remember I bought two Rolex watches there off my mate based in Southend called David Chapman. He used to advertise in the *Exchange and Mart*. I bought two gold Day-Date diamond-set watches off him. She had the ladies one with a diamond set and bracelet. I had the one with a diamond-bezel face. I even commissioned him to make a bracelet full of diamonds, which cost me a few bob. When people saw them on the island they started calling me 'the diamond fella'.

And it didn't stop there. Most days we'd be out shopping in Colchester. After spending a fortune on designer clothes we'd go and have lunch and get drunk. Then it was back to the house and on to the gear, if we hadn't already had a few lines in the restaurant toilet. We became regulars in quite a few restaurants around the area. I used to go to this posh French restaurant in Colchester called Le Talbooth. We got friendly with some of the staff, so much so that I nearly got the head waiter sacked one night. His name was Mutash and he was from the Seychelles. He had a big moustache and used to look like one of the Dolmio characters. One night I got him really drunk and took him back to a hotel room where he had some gear. He got so smashed he forgot to turn the alarms off, and they all went off the next day. The owner went mad and nearly sacked him. I remember when he realised what had happened, he panicked and started crying. We managed to smooth things over in the end but I bet that's the last time he ever touched the powder.

Lay and Wheeler used to do themed nights, which I often went along to. I went in there one Christmas on a Chinese-themed night with my nephew, and spent £1,500 on Krug and Crystal Rose. I always used to say I was buying Cristal as an investment but instead I'd drink it by the case-load. I've always been a generous man, and never shied away from tipping staff. I was very brash at this stage of my life, so I was giving away money like it was going out of fashion. At most restaurants I used to give all the staff a £20 tip. Understandably they loved me for it, and used to queue up for it as I left. I would never shy away from spending money, either. I took a bloke to Le Talbooth one night with his wife and the bill was £800. He framed it in the end. At the time he was devastated. He went, "I've brought out £300 with me." I said,

"What are you worrying about, I'll get it." I used to go in there on a regular basis, spending stupid amounts of money.

While I was squandering my hard-earned fortune, the auction house remained shut. It was drink and drugs that set me back. I think it might have done all right, but I'd got into the party scene. Things got so heavy that I collapsed a couple of times. The ambulance came out after I went all funny. I'd overdosed because I did so much gear. It's was an explosion of emotions. You don't know where you are. Your heart's coming out of your chest. You're thinking constantly, "Am I going to be all right?" You're thinking any minute, "I'm going to drop dead." The ambulance came, the paramedics looked at me and didn't even take me away. They said, "Just sit down and calm down." They can't really give you anything. Sometimes they give you insulin or sugar.

I got so involved in the drink and drugs that nothing else mattered. We had plans to do loads of things, but they never happened because we were constantly buzzing off our tits. To this day I still can't say why. She even wanted to turn it into a restaurant. I had another one of my crazy plans to sell concrete garden furniture out of it. I went to a company in Sittingbourne and spent £2,000 on the stuff. It was the biggest company in England for that stuff and I had loads of frogs, gnomes and statues of naked woman lying around.

Like with my other plans at that place, nothing ever happened, and we gave them away in the end. Weekends got out on control. You're so fucked over the weekend that Monday comes round and you're still fucked. You're not going to go to work. You lie in bed for hours in the afternoon, recovering. You think "I'm never going to do that again." Then the next day comes and you have another line.

I wasted a lot more cash when I got involved with a friend who was running soul nights up the West End. They were old-school nights and I put in about £4,000 a week. He was selling the tickets, but the money never came in. He was an addict himself, and frequently got drunk and went missing. We fell out in the end and I came away from him, but not before I'd forked out thousands of pounds for nothing.

The only thing I did down there that was any success was selling cars. After I had a bit of success with Mercedes I started selling long-wheelbase Mitsubishi Shoguns. They weren't cheap, and kept getting electrical problems, but I used to fix them up and sell them on. That house had a double garage, so I looked like a genuine seller. They were really popular in the late '90s so I was selling them like hot cakes, and all the profit was cash. That might sound like a good thing, but in reality it meant that the minute I made a sale I was ringing my dealer to get some more gear in.

Throughout all of this, things were still tense with Karen, and I was almost glad when the landlord said she was selling up so we had to leave. The wife was all right but the geezer was a bit of a wanker. I don't think they wanted to sell it, I think they wanted us out. A bloke across the road complained that I was having a few parties there. I had a few words with him, nothing violent, just verbal. But he was one of those Captain Mannering types who was a member of West Mersea Sailing Club. When I told him to fuck off he said, "You're the wide boy with the auction room round the corner." I told him where to go after that, and I think he went and complained to the landlord. Shortly after that they said they wanted us out. To me it wasn't a coincidence, but looking back it was probably a blessing in disguise. I was getting far too heavy on the gear and booze there, and doing myself some real damage.

I'd always prided myself on being a switched-on fella, but none of my plans ever materialised there. When we eventually left it was very sad because the Treasure Island signs were still up.

My friend Keith, the one whose dad was a copper, worked as an estate agent, and when I told him we were looking for somewhere new he got us a house round the corner in Victory Lane. It was smaller, and £900 a month, but it would do as a stop-gap. We signed a six-month contract and moved in straightaway. The drinking and drug-taking carried on, but by that point the writing was on the wall. Tensions were running high with a lot of people on the island, and I was getting funny looks off people. I think they thought I was some sort of East End gangster, which I've never been. It's a weird place where everyone knows each other, and rumours spread like wildfire. That certainly happened in my case, so in the end I thought "Let's get the fuck out of here" after a couple of months. I'd signed up for six months so it wasn't a great rush, but I knew I had to plan for our next adventure.

CHAPTER 13
—
VENICE

We were constantly rowing about a load of old bollocks, and I thought I needed to do something about this. Instead of moving, I thought going on holiday would solve all our problems. I'm not sure why I picked Venice but I said to her one day: "Fuck all this, let's go to Italy." She agreed, so we arranged for my parents to have the kids. We booked it last-minute, so the only place I could get a flight to Milan was from Manchester. We drove off up north in an Audi convertible I bought off the geezer I was doing the promotion night stuff with in the West End. He was a bit dodgy but it seemed like a good car for £6,000, so I took it.

When we got to Manchester we couldn't get a room for love or money. Manchester United was playing so there were no hotel rooms. We ended up staying in the car, where we had a bit of gear to keep us going. I put my alarm on my phone but, as you can imagine, we had a terrible night's sleep. When we woke up it was really close to the flight's departure, so we sprinted to the point where you get the bus to the terminal.

I was wearing all my Louise Vuitton gear and even had a Louis Vuitton man bag before everyone else had them. My son's still got it. He said the reason he's kept it is because it's had more money in it than the Bank of England, and more coke in it than Pablo Escobar's drugs factory. I bought it from the shop in Bond Street, and used to take it everywhere.

As we got on the bus we were sweating like we're on Death Row. It took us to the airport and when we got off I said to Karen, "Where's my Louis Vuitton bag?" It had about £35,000 in it. It turned out I'd left it on the roof of the car. I went to get back on the bus and said to the driver, "I've left my Louis Vuitton bag on the roof of my car with £35,000 in." Why I told him that I don't know, I just panicked. He immediately got on the radio and said,

"There's a bloke here who's left his bag on top of an Audi car with £35,000 in." I thought, "Why's he told them that?" Then it clicked: I had to get to that car sharpish.

I weighed about 17 stone at the time, but I promise you, I ran back to that car like Linford Christie. I got within sight of the car and the bag was on the roof. Thankfully the money was still there. I collected it and got back to the airport just in time to catch the flight. We were the last ones to board, and everyone was waiting. I'd had a bit of gear that Karen sneaked on board inside her bra, so I didn't give a fuck about the dirty looks. I was off my tits.

When we got to Italy we spent a day in Milan. I went on a shopping spree and bought a Louis Vuitton sunglasses case for £400 and an Yves St Laurent mac coat for about £2,000. The first night we got bang on the drink and gear. I was drinking Dom Perignon and talking bollocks to a load of Germans in there. I had a pink Gucci shirt on with blue trousers and blue suede shoes. I looked like fucking Elvis Presley when he was fat. I had my diamond-encrusted watch and all that shit. The second day we went out I bought Karen a £2,000 Versace pink top. I went into the main store in Milan and she found that pink chiffon silk top, tied round the neck, that was really classy. I bought a pair of trousers and a few other things. When I went to pay the bloke said to me at the counter, "Are you paying in pounds sterling?" I said I was, and he gave me a £6,000 bill. I nearly had a heart attack. "At least the complimentary coffee wasn't bad," I thought.

That night we went out and got heavily on the drink. The coke Karen sneaked on the plane didn't last long, but it wasn't an issue getting some more. Like I've always said, if you know how to approach people you can always score. We might not have spoken the same language, but some bloke sorted me a bit of gear in a bar in Milan. It's rife over there, but then what do you expect – it's the fashion capital of Europe, and catwalk models are famous for taking the powder. Being a heavily overweight man at the time, I wasn't taking it to maintain my physique, but I enjoyed it all the same.

The next morning, we got an old-fashioned wooden boat to Venice where we stayed in the Baglioni for four nights. It was £960 a night, and brought a new meaning to the word posh. They even give you complimentary slippers and dressing gowns. When you're having a meal there are always four people standing there in case you drop something. When you drop a crumb they get a dustpan. You feel like a 15th-century lord, and it was too much for me.

After dinner, we went to Harry's bar in Venice. It's famous for its dry martinis, and has been visited by the likes of George Clooney and Woody Allen. I went in there all guns blazing and bought champagne and cocktails for half the bar. That set me back about £2,000 but I didn't care, I was coked up and had money to burn. It shut at 11pm, so afterwards we were looking for somewhere else to go. As we went to leave I realised I'd lost my bag again. It had about £4,000, and I was panicking because I didn't have any other cash on me. The only place it could be was in the hotel, so I ran back up to the suite looking like an Italian gigolo with all my designer clobber. I got inside and found the bag and the £4,000 on the bedside without a penny missing. I realised that the cleaner had picked the money up and put it out of the way without taking a penny.

I appreciate that sort of honesty. To me it's like gold dust, so I went to the lobby and asked who had been cleaning my room. A woman came over and I went to give her £300. Her manager saw it and said, "If she takes some money, she loses her job." It's that strict there. They ran it like an army battalion, and if the staff stepped a foot wrong they got sacked on the spot. I didn't really care about that though, and was still determined to show this woman my gratitude. Before I left I bumped into her and gave her £300 very slyly under the table. She said, "Thank you very much, I'll give it to my family."

With the £4,000 back in my pocket we carried on partying in the bars around Venice before heading back to the Baglioni in the early hours to carry on drinking. We managed to score a bit of gear out there, but we got more on the champagne. I was drinking Grand Vintage Krug, which cost £600 a bottle. It was very moreish, which you'd expect for that price.

We met a few characters in the hotel bar, including an Old Bailey judge. He had some pretty blonde bird who looked about 30 years younger than him. I'll never forget, he wasn't wearing socks, had a checkered tweed jacket and a cravat. He looked like a proper old English gent, all he was missing was a shotgun and a pipe. I was sitting there out of my nut speaking to them when he told me what he did. He then said, "I'm sure I've seen you somewhere." I replied, "You haven't seen me, mate," before I made my excuses and slipped off.

I spent so much money in the bars that I put all our drinks on a tab at the hotel. On the last night, the bartender came up to me and asked me to settle the bill. He said, "There's no rush, sir, whenever you are ready." When I walked over and saw the amount, I needed another drink. It was over £3,000. Even though I took £35,000 with me, I'd spent it all and couldn't pay. I didn't have a credit card so I had to get my dad to wire me through another £7,000 by Western Union. He went to a dodgy corner shop to do it and I was sweating the whole time, hoping nothing went wrong. It didn't, so to celebrate I went and spent a small fortune in Prada. I came out looking like a 20-stone Italian gigolo. I had a pair of cream trousers that made me look like a penguin. I even grew a little moustache, which didn't suit me. They'd have sectioned me in the UK if I walked around looking like that. But I didn't care, I was off my nut.

After Prada I went to Brioni, another high-end boutique that costs you an arm and a leg. In there a plain white shirt sets you back £1,100. T-shirts aren't quite as dear, at £800 a pop. When I went in there and the bloke behind the till laughed at my Prada clobber and said, "you don't want to be wearing clothes like that, you look ridiculous." I showed him my Rolex and he said, "That's rubbish. You don't want those dodgy diamond Rolexes. People with style wear Patek Philippe watches." I thought "You cheeky bastard", but after we had a bit of banter he turned out to be a nice fella. He convinced me to buy a blue shirt, a pair of brown trousers and a leather jacket for £4,500. I came out of there looking like Prince Charles. I even bought three pairs of leather trainers for £1,200 each. I liked them so much I went back to Venice a couple of years later to buy five more pairs.

With all my new clothes we headed to the airport, red as lobsters, and looking forward to putting our feet up when we got home. All I wanted to do when I got back to Manchester was get in the car and go home. But when we arrived we soon discovered the car was missing. The airport staff told me it had been towed away and said I should contact the police. I did, and the next thing I know two officers come down and nicked me. They said the car was stolen, and arrested me on suspicion of theft. My mate sold me a ringer without telling me, the bastard.

The police were pretty fair at first, despite calling me a 'Cockney bastard'. I just told them, "I don't know what you're talking about. I bought it in good faith." I then went "No comment" and they took me down the station at Manchester airport, where they held me for two days. When I got arrested I handed my two Rolexes and diamond bracelet in. That raised a few eyebrows, and they thought I was some London gangster after that. I knew they didn't like me when a CID officer came up to me and said, "We don't want any of you Cockney wide boys up here. Don't even fucking come up here again, I know what you're all about." I said, "What are you trying to insinuate?" He said, "You're a wide boy from London, we don't want your sort round here."

I could tell they were getting frustrated when I hadn't made a comment or signed a statement for two days. On the second day two coppers, a stocky younger guy and his skinnier older mate, came in to interview me. It was in the cell without a lawyer, which I'm sure isn't legal. The second they came in the atmosphere turned nasty. From the off they wanted an argument. They said, "The case is pending, we're going to keep the car." I said, "You're fucking joking." They then accused me of not cooperating or making a statement. I told them to fuck off.

That's when they pounced and pinned me down. I was struggling, and headbutted one of them in the face. After that they both went ballistic and had me on the floor, kicking the shit out of me. The younger one pinned me down while the older one repeatedly punched me in the ribs. Karen was next door, and she told me later she heard all the screaming and shouting. I was having a good go back, and because I was buzzing I didn't feel the pain. It went on for a good few minutes before they left go. All my shirt was ripped but I stood my ground even if I was on the losing side. I didn't have much of a chance when there were two of them. The next day I was covered in bruises. I think they broke two of my ribs as well, but I'll never know for sure because I never went to hospital. After they'd kicked the shit out of me they took us to another police station near Manchester city centre, where I was released. I was determined to get home so I went up to the nearest black cab rank and said, "Will you take me to West Mersea?" The driver said, "Where's that?" I said, "Essex." He agreed and said, "Are you all right, you look terrible?" I told him I'd had a terrible run-in, so I went and got a cup of tea and sat in the back with Karen. He turned the meter off in the end and said, "I'll charge you £300." I gave him a £70 tip for sorting me out, and was just happy to get home.

During the journey he asked me what had happened. I was a bit reluctant to tell him at first, but eventually I said, "I've had a bit of trouble with the Old Bill over my car." He said, "You should have told me. My dad's the superintendant of Greater Manchester Police." After that I didn't speak to him the whole way back.

When I got to West Mersea my parents said they'd had the police round at 3am, raiding the house looking for stolen cars. Nothing was there and they probably just did it to piss me off. Before the driver left, my mum offered him a cup of tea. I was going, "No, don't let him in the house, his dad's a copper." Not that he'd done anything wrong, in fact he was a nice guy, but I wanted to stay clear of anyone connected to the police at that point. When he left I shook his hand and he said, "That's the best fare I've ever had or am likely to get. No one's ever got a black cab from Manchester airport to Essex." Sitting back at the house, I thought: "I've done more than £40,000, lost my car and had the shit kicked out of me." What a holiday!

A few days later the police rang up and offered me the car back. I spoke to the insurance company and it turned out it was twinned with another stolen car. They said, "We'll do you a deal, but you've got to change the registration plates." I didn't want anything to do with that car, and said, "Bollocks, just give me the money." Karen had the hump because I'd bought her that car and she wanted to keep it. I wasn't having any of it: it attracted bad luck, and I wanted it gone.

CHAPTER 14

—

LEAVING
WEST MERSEA

We got back to the house in Victory Lane, but things still weren't good between us. There was no business to run, and neither of us were doing anything apart from getting fucked. Taking that amount of coke and drinking like a fish is no way to live, especially when you've got two young kids. You think you're going to put a business together but it doesn't materialise because you say, "I'll do it tomorrow." When tomorrow comes you think "Fuck it, I'll leave it and have a drink." Everything is great. The music is on, you are dancing away, people are round and you're having your turn out in the bedroom.

When you come back round to reality, it's a very sad place to be. It's a reality check, so you go clean for a couple of days. But when you have two days of normality you think "Fuck, this isn't much fun." You see your kids are unhappy, your business is failing and your relationship is going down the pan. "I'm letting things slip, what the fuck is going on?" you say to yourself. You know you've got to pull myself together but then bang, Mr Coke knocks on the door and it's back to the party scene. "Don't worry about that," you say. "I'll get that. Let's go and spend a few quid." Eventually you're going to crash, whether you're Bill Gates or Bob Smith from down the road. Whenever I had the crashes I used to think: "Let's move and start somewhere fresh."

It had been a very bad experience living on West Mersea. I was using loads of gear, drinking like a fish, overweight, and in a bad place in my mind. She used to cook, but the wine was constantly flowing. We used to have those bowl glasses. You could drink three bottles of wine a night, no problem. I was drinking Le Montrachet wine, which even 15 years ago was £120 a bottle. I'd always have Krug Grande Cuvée champagne too, which was pricey. You can't get it out of Tesco Express, you have to go to a proper wine brokers and they sell it in cases. I'd gone "Fuck it, I'll take six cases." That's 36 bottles of wine, and I'd go there every week. It meant that there was a constant supply of booze to binge on. And whenever we started drinking, the coke would always follow.

Eventually things came to a head down in West Mersea. The kids were suffering. It was no way for them to be brought up. We'd send them to bed, just so we could carry on drinking and taking gear. I sat there on my own many times doing a bit of gear, which is a very difficult thing to admit. Sitting there by yourself having a drink and doing a line, that's when you're truly an addict. Your mind is all over the place, wandering in and out of terrible thoughts. Your sexual desires get extreme. You have delusions about being the biggest gangster in the world or the richest businessman in Great Britain. You think you're a genius who's going to be on the rich list. Then bang, your heartbeat is up because you've had too much coke and you start panicking. You're not thinking you're the biggest man in the world any more, you're just hoping you don't keel over and die. "Have another glass of wine," you think. "That'll calm things down."

That works, but then you fuck yourself again by having another two lines. So you're up, down, up, down. All of a sudden you crash. And when you crash, it's a terrible feeling. There's no gear left, and you're desperate for some. Your feel as though your world has come to an end. Your dreams are shattered. You look upstairs at your family and feel shame. Children come into it a lot.

When your kids are young they look up to you like their hero. Heroes don't go into the toilet and sniff coke. Your son is looking at you saying, there's my dad. You're fucked out your nut, you can't even talk. It's dreadful. You give them £100 to keep them quiet when you should be spending quality time together. It's a regrettable action that can never be repaired. You just live with it day to day, and make amends the best you can. Luckily enough my sons are sensible and I think that's a thing of the past. But it's a terrible thing.

You don't see your children grow up. You should help them do their homework, and play with them. It was never for me, I was too wrapped up in my own world of being something that I wasn't as the coke took over. Your personality is stolen, and the coke and drink are in control. I always tried to look after my family the best way I could even though I was a coke-head. But it isn't about giving them money. How about cuddling your kids, going to the school fetes and school plays, and making cakes with them. That never happened and it's something I regret to this day.

They never went to school anyway and most of the time I was in bed, drunk, buzzing off my nut, talking for England or rushing about here and there, too busy to notice that. Instead of being with my kids I'd be sitting with undesirable strangers, talking shit. Both my sons are clean from what I gather. They might have the odd drink, but they've seen what devastation cocaine causes and it has scolded them. In a way I'm glad, but it's probably put a barrier up, and they're going "No way am I going near that shit." They've had a tough upbringing and learned a lot. They've had the luxuries, which is irrelevant because you can't replace love. You can't give your kid £100 to go and play on the Playstation while you sit downstairs and do a bit of gear. You should sit downstairs and play with them. I never did that, and I feel terrible about it. It's heart-breaking, to be honest.

But they got through it, and they stood by me. I'm close with them now, and train with them, so at least something good might come out of it.

After five months in the second house in West Mersea, I said "We've got to get out of here immediately." Everything was falling apart. I thanked Keith for sorting me out with the house, and we left in a hurry. All we had to do now was find somewhere to live. I'd blown more than £150,000 in a year, so I was no longer capable of living the same kind of lifestyle. I wasn't a pauper, and could still afford a comfortable standard of living by most people's standards.

But it wasn't like before, and I knew it.

CHAPTER 15

—

STOWMARKET

I'd often go for drives out into the sticks, just to have a look. It was on one of these that I visited Stowmarket, a little town in Suffolk. It's only an hour's drive from West Mersea but the towns are worlds apart. Moving there and setting up a business would help me fix all my problems, I said to myself.

With that in my mind I found a five-bed barn conversion just outside Stowmarket for about £800 a month. It was really rural and had recently been renovated so it was nicely kitted out, and had all the original beams.

With Karen being a fully qualified beautician I thought running a beauty parlour would make money and bring us closer together. It was a foolproof plan, I thought. All I needed now was a shop to put the business in. That didn't take long. I saw a big empty shop in the high street and immediately contacted the landlord. It was only £100 a week, so I agreed terms and got the keys. All I needed to do now was to buy the equipment to run the place, like sun beds and nail varnish. I went to an Olympia Beauty exhibition at the NEC in Birmingham and spent about £15,000 on kit. We decked out the shop, which I called Tropical Nail and Beauty Clinic, and opened a few days later.

To ensure everyone in Suffolk knew I was opening a business I employed my old tricks of paying scantily dressed girls in tight tops to hand balloons and vouchers out. I undercut everyone and had signs written on all my cars. It was like with the pine shops, people got sick to death of hearing about it. But it worked, and I had streams of people coming in – blokes and women.

It was buzzing, and we were making a fortune. Unfortunately, I don't think they'd ever seen anything like it in Suffolk, and the parish council went ballistic. It immediately caused mayhem, and I thought the locals were going to turn up with pitchforks and burn me at the stake. The parish council chairman apparently said, "That wide boy down there. We need to get him out." They even started a petition to get rid of me. They might have hated me, but I was making a killing. Within weeks of opening I was taking £4,000 a week. It did so well that within months I opened another shop in Needham Market, just down the road. This was followed swiftly by a sunbed shop called Tropical Tanning.

Things were going so well that I branched out into selling diet pills called Thermoslimmers, which were made by a company called Cados. I put a little box advert in the newspaper saying 'weight loss, seven-day plan'. Overnight I had a queue of overweight middle-aged women banging on my door, demanding a six-month plan. I was happy to oblige and was turning over £2,000 a week off the pills alone. My little earner didn't go unnoticed by the local town copper, who couldn't stand me. He came in one day and asked to buy some for his wife. I thought he was lying and they were for him, because he could do with losing a few pounds himself. What he actually did was send them off to a lab to get tested. He thought I was selling speed, the bastard. I wasn't and they were all legal – much to his disappointment, I was later told.

With the business ticking over I thought I was back in the game and imagined opening more shops in other towns. That gave me itchy feet and I wanted to celebrate and go out more. I couldn't do that where we were living because it was in the middle nowhere. It was a nice place but we soon got tired of not living around other people. I couldn't just walk to the pub because it was five miles away.

Around this time the flat above the shop in Needham Market became vacant, and the landlord agreed to let us have the whole place for not much more than we were already paying. It was a beautiful old listed building with the original décor, and more than enough space for the four of us. It was a lovely place, but living back in a town meant temptation was only a stone's throw away.

Unfortunately, we weren't strong enough to resist and very quickly we got back heavily on the coke and booze. Some people think that getting drugs out in small rural towns is hard. They couldn't be more wrong. I could walk into a sweet shop in North Wales and come out with some smack if I wanted to. The key is knowing how to talk to people, and approaching them in the right way. Needham Market was full of drugs, like most places, and as our consumption went up I started getting involved with a few plastic gangsters who thought they were Al Capone because they sold two grams of coke down the pub on a Friday night. I even started buying it off customers who came into the shop.

I remember a mixed-race girl came in with her boyfriend one day. They looked like they'd had a heavy night and we got chatting. He said he got on the gear, and linked me up. It went from there and he'd sorted me out a couple of grams within half an hour.

It might have been easy to get out there, but it was heavily cut stuff. London has the best gear, and the further you go away from the capital, the worse it gets. The expression is 'trod on', which means people mix in stuff like Pro Plus and talcum powder to maximise their profits. It might be 60 per cent pure in London if you pay a premium, but by the time the carrot-crunchers in Norfolk get their hands on it it's probably down to 10 per cent maximum. Not only is it weaker, a lot of the time it blocks your sinuses, which is never nice. If I ever fancied something a bit purer I'd drive back to London and meet a dealer I knew at the M25 services. That was a rarity, though, and for the most part I just mooched around between the shops thinking I was back in business.

Unfortunately I wasn't, and things really took a turn for the worse when we got the eight girls we had working for us on the powder. They were all locals, and to start with Karen was doing a good job running the place. But moving in upstairs meant the gear was only 20 feet away at all times. We started getting friendlier with them, and would often invite them upstairs for a line or two after work. Those odds lines regularly turned into heavy sessions which lasted until the early hours. As we got back on the powder the business slipped, and we'd be so fucked in the morning we often didn't open up on time. Some of the staff weren't up to it, and Karen had to let them go. It was the right thing to do but it put more pressure on us, and made things get even sloppier.

With the business failing, we quickly started to get bad vibes between each other. We'd been married little more than a year and it was supposed to be a fresh start, but that never happened. We started having a few disagreements over trivial things that blew up and turned into a massive row. Instead of facing up to my problems I kept on using, and buried my head in the sand by spending erratically and getting out of my nut. My mood swings were terrible and it wasn't a nice experience for anyone, especially the boys who were only five and seven.

The money continued to go down and I couldn't see a light at the end of the tunnel. We'd been there little more than a year and already takings were falling. In towns like that word gets round pretty quick, and people heard about the drug-taking and the erratic owners. It wasn't exactly a family-friendly image, and that put people off.

With things slipping, I had another bit of bad news that hit me for six. A very good friend of mine committed suicide. His name was Mike, and I'd known him since I was a kid in East London. He blew his head off in front of his two boys with a revolver. They were only seven and nine. As always, it was to do with the powder. He was a property developer, and got into debt over a business deal. It all stemmed from him not keeping things under control because he was such a heavy coke user. He'd been in trouble for a while, and was burying his head in the powder instead of dealing with reality. I'm not judging him, because I've done exactly the same thing.

The story goes that he was having an argument with his wife about how they were going to cope at their house in Basildon. He said, "If you keep going on I'll go upstairs, get my gun and shoot myself." She apparently replied, "do what you want." He called her bluff, went up and got the gun and came back down. In front of their kids, he put it under his chin and pulled the trigger. There's a rumour that he didn't know it was loaded and it was just an act to scare her. I personally don't know what to believe and the only person who knows what really happened is Mike, who is tragically dead. Like with Steve's death, I didn't cope with the news well and broke down. I should have seen that his death was down to the coke, but I was so blinded by my addiction that I couldn't. As ever, it should have been a wake-up call, but predictably it wasn't, and I buried my own head in a mountain of powder.

My state of mind meant the business was slipping even more. I didn't bother to go into work for weeks after Mike died, and it was on the brink of collapse when it really started to implode. Not long after Mike died it was my birthday, so we went out to a Chinese in Witham to celebrate. During the meal I got chatting to one of our nail technicians, a 20-year-old girl called Sophie. She was a pretty, short girl with dark hair and big tits who thought she knew it all. In reality, she couldn't put a kettle on. We got on the gear and she told me she'd be interested in buying the business. I remember thinking "Bollocks love, you haven't got a penny to your name." I was right, but she had a rich boyfriend who was wrapped round her finger. She might have looked adorable but she had a nasty streak, and she was taking this poor bloke to the cleaners.

After that night she kept on at me about buying the clinics, so eventually I said, "Bring your boyfriend round and we can talk." The next day, when he turned up I couldn't believe it. I went outside to see this 20-stone geezer in his 50s who looked like he hadn't washed since 1994. All his clothes were stained, and even the leather on his shoes was flapping off. I thought he was Bernard Matthews' brother to start with. I wasn't far wrong, because it turned out he was a chicken farmer from Norfolk. There was no way she was with him for his looks, I'm 100 per cent sure about that. His appearance might not have shown it, but he had money. He turned up in a brand-new silver Porsche 911 Turbo, which didn't even have number plates. His name was Alan and he told me the plates were in the footwell because he'd just bought it. We got chatting and I said I wanted £40,000 for the business. To my surprise he offered to pay me £35,000 for it, and he told me Sophie was going to run it. "Good luck with that," I thought.

She had no idea how to run a business but that wasn't my concern, I just wanted out of there. The next day he came down and handed me a filthy, scrunched-up bit of paper that looked like someone had blown their nose with it. I thought "This is a con" and was very dubious. I went down to NatWest bank and the cashier said, "It's a genuine banker's draft, but it'll take few days to go through." I was over the moon, and within a month we'd completely cleared out of there.

Sophie promptly took over, and apparently ran the business into the ground within six weeks. She had no idea what she was doing, and was just a loudmouth. I feel sorry for him because he was a nice guy and she took him for a mug. Unfortunately, that can happen all too easily unless you keep your wits about you.

CHAPTER 16

—

MOVING
TO KENT

After Needham Market I stupidly thought that moving would improve the situation. By this point my parents had left the Isle of Dogs and moved to a place in Faversham, Kent. It's called Browntown because it's full of smackheads, so I didn't fancy living there.

They hadn't been there long when my mum was diagnosed with breast cancer. She had a mastectomy, but she was still very weak and I wanted to be closer to her. She was looking very gaunt and fragile. It was dreadful to see, but when someone you love gets cancer, what can you do? You're powerless, and that just makes things even worse. I didn't take the news well, and worried about what was going to happen. I'd always had my mum there, and the thought of her not being a guiding influence really hurt me.

With the £35,000 from the sale and a bit more cash stashed away, all I needed to do was find somewhere nice. We were looking around the area for somewhere when I saw a house for rent in Sellindge, Kent. It's a little village about a ten-minute drive from Ashford, Kent. At £950 a month it wasn't cheap for 2006, but it was a nice place so we went for it. I remember the landlord was getting a bit funny about references, so to shut him up I paid a year's rent upfront. I said, "There you go mate. There's £10,000 cash." I remember walking down the high street in Ashford with the money in my bag.

After we moved in, I didn't do a lot of start with. There were no obvious business ventures so I just mucked about. I had excess money to live off, so it wasn't a problem. I was still doing the gear and drinking like you have cups of tea, but it wasn't as rancid as before. I was getting through hundreds of pounds a week but, compared with before, it was quite conservative. I had that little bit of money, so I think mentally I wasn't as stressed about making a pound note.

With nothing to do I thought "Let's go on holiday." Egypt was the up-and-coming place at the time, so I took the four of us to a five-star hotel over there for three weeks. It was in Sharm El Sheikh – a resort town between the desert of the Sinai Peninsula and the Red Sea. The place had just been built and was absolutely beautiful, with gold everywhere. I paid £8,000 and we got everything inclusive. The hotel had a varied menu, so instead of going for steak, eggs and chips I thought I'd broaden my horizons and taste the local cuisine. That turned out to be a big mistake, and some dodgy meat I tried gave me terrible food poisoning. Thankfully it wasn't terminal, and after a couple of days on the toilet I was back up and running.

Now I was feeling better, the only thing I needed was a bit of gear, and it didn't take me long to find it. I managed to get some on the third day after I befriended one of the waiters. His English wasn't too good so I mimed sniffing a line and he immediately said, "Yes, yes, yes." Within 20 minutes he'd sorted me out a couple of grams. The coke out there wasn't like the stuff you get here. It was fucking damp yellow stuff that smelt like it had been cut with diesel. But it worked. Just a line of it gave me heart palpitations, and sent me completely off my head. It was cheap as chips too at £10 a gram, so you couldn't really complain.

The holiday was meant to be a distraction from my mother's illness, and a chance for me and Karen to get back on good terms. For a brief moment it actually worked, and we had our close moments. I was happy spending time with my family and seeing the boys running around having a laugh and jumping in the pool. Sadly, it wasn't to last and things felt distant when we got back to the UK. Our relationship got even more frayed when she started constantly going to a fitness club nearby. Things were right between us and something was going on. She started going missing for hours on end without any explanation. She'd always say she was down the gym, but I knew something was going on. We were drifting apart more and more every day. Looking back I knew we should never have got back together, but at the time it never clicked.

With nothing to do I constantly wondered what she was doing, which made me feel even worse. To give me something to do I started selling a few cars again. I'd go down to British Car Auctions and look for things I could flog on. It wasn't mega money but I did all right selling them on, and thought "I'm on to something here."

Around the same time I had my next business idea. I spotted a big hangar for rent one night when I was driving into Sellindge. It was a 30-second drive from the house so it was a perfect location. It was owned by 'Big Bob', a mechanic who ran a garage next door. He was a right country bumpkin who was always saying things like "All right boi." He had size 16 boots but didn't know what day it was. He went to me, "It's £100 a week" and I took it on the spot. Initially I ran a car wash there, but it never kicked off because it wasn't busy enough, so I shut it down pretty sharpish. I wondered what I could replace it with when I thought about going back into scrap. It was a very big site and you could easily fit two articulated lorries inside. I asked Bob if he minded me doing a bit of scrap. When he said he didn't I contacted Avery, the company that makes the scales, and got cracking.

What I hadn't realised was that things had changed since I did scrap with my father in the 1980s. By this point it was all digital. Back in my day it was imperial, and we used hundredweights. That wasn't a big issue though, and I quickly had a set of four-tonne scales which came on a great big platform. It was about the size of four square pallets, so you could throw metal on and it would weigh it up. As soon as I opened I started taking money. There weren't any other scrap dealers that close, so people came from all over. I was happy to pay cash and didn't mess people around, so everything ticked over nicely. But I quickly discovered that I had another much bigger problem.

The law had changed since I stopped doing scrap, and you now needed a metal licence. Years before, when I was with my dad, you could open anywhere. All you needed was a set of scales and money to pay people. By the mid 2000s they had changed the law to combat metal theft and control waste from battery acid. When I realised I'd have to shut without a licence I thought "This isn't going to happen." It was a real shame because I was just getting the business going, and that stopped it in its tracks. As a desperate last throw of the dice I applied to the council for a licence, because I thought: "It's worth a final punt." I didn't hold out much hope but would you believe it, they gave me one. Scrap metal licences are as rare as rocking-horse shit and they gave me one. Normally you've got to be with the council to get one but I'd managed to blag myself one with no connections. I think a lack of scrap dealers in the area was my saving grace.

The minute I got the licence, I framed it and put it up on the wall. I thought I'd be there for years. I even started selling a few cars from there. I was specialising in 4 x 4 Cherokee Jeeps. They were P and R regs with all the leather. It was topping up my wage by £1,000 a week, so I couldn't complain. With the business heading in the right direction I even started to feel better in myself. I'd taken a bit of a knock in West Mersea and Suffolk, and I was back to doing what I liked most – using my initiative to chase a pound note. The business was all going tickety-boo, and I know

I would have done well there. Then something happened that put me on a real downer.

I'd had a fall-out with Julie's husband Ian about some old bollocks, so I told him to fuck off. He didn't take it too well and kept ringing me saying "I need to talk to you." I was in one of my moods, so I ignored him and went about my day. The next thing I know my Julie's is calling me crying her eyes out. She was so hysterical that I couldn't work out what she was saying at first. Finally, she blurted out, "I've had the British Transport Police round. Ian's dead. He jumped in front of a train at Raleigh Station." It didn't register at first, and then I couldn't believe it was true. I'd only spoken to him a day earlier, when he was his usual jolly giant self. Then it all clicked. He's come to the end of his tether, that's why he kept ringing me.

From that moment, I knew it was coke-related. It had to be, because he'd had a problem with it for years. Ian had an addictive personality, and went from having two lines to spending £500 on the stuff every week in the blink of an eye. I know, because I used to do it with him when he worked for me in my furniture shops years earlier. When they did the post mortem it confirmed what I feared. They found all sorts of drugs in his body, including cocaine. At his inquest they said he'd parked his van up near the station and locked it with all his stuff in, including his wallet. He then went and hid in the bushes while he waited for a train to come. When he finally stood in front of a train, the driver said he saw him running away as it was hurtling down the track. No one knows why he did that. Maybe he had a last-minute change of heart, but sadly it was too late by then.

I'll never know or understand why he did it. He left my sister and seven kids behind without a husband or father. I know he'd had troubles with Julie in the past, but what marriage doesn't? The only explanation I can think of is that drugs got the better of him. It should have been a wake-up call for me to stop taking coke, just like Steve and Mike's deaths were. But it wasn't, and I kept on burying my head in a mountain of powder.

Ian's death hit me much harder than I realised at the time. I was under a lot of stress because of what was going on at home, and losing him made everything a thousand times worse. At the same time, things were coming to a head with Karen. Instead of facing my problems head-on, I thought the best option was to move. I convinced myself for the hundredth time that moving would improve my life. If only that was true!

The dust hadn't even settled on the licence frame when we left. We'd been in Sellindge for about a year, and my home life was rapidly falling apart. It seemed like Karen was constantly out without me, not telling me where she was going. The more she went missing, the more we argued. It wasn't just about the coke, although I was using it to delude myself. We weren't happy together, and were beginning to really dislike each other. We didn't like spending time in each other's company, which is a bad sign in any marriage. When you've just started going out, it's easy to walk away. But if you're married, live together and have got two kids, it's a different kettle of fish. It could have fallen apart, but I was still determined to make it work. I didn't want my kids to grow up in a broken home, and I kept that thought at the back of my mind.

While I tried to make it work, I buried my head in a mountain of coke. I had good money coming in, so late nights on the powder and drink became a regular fixture again as I tried to distract

144

myself from my crumbling marriage. Karen never turned down a line, to be fair. We'd be all lovey-dovey one moment, only to be at each other's throats the next. A full-blown row could kick off at a moment's notice. Normally it was about where she'd been. She'd always have a convenient explanation, but I knew she was talking bollocks. Something was up. I don't know if she was playing away, but things weren't right and I thought the only option was to move.

Even when I handed the keys back, I thought this might be a mistake. It fucking was. I could have made a lot of money there, because I knew the scrap metal business back to front from my father. I even got on with my landlord for a change, and Big Bob was happy for me to crack away with my business. It was a missed opportunity.

But like always, the powder and the drink dragged me away from an open goal.

CHAPTER 17

—

BACK TO
EAST ANGLIA

After Sellindge we just looked around to rent or buy in Kent, but it was so dear that I wanted to move further afield. It wasn't just about money: I wanted to make a fresh start. It was a big mistake, because your problems always follow you.

One weekend we were in Great Yarmouth, when I stumbled across Gorleston. I had no reason to go there, apart from just to get away from my problems. I used to like calling myself Lord Lucan. Gorleston was a quiet seaside town, and seemed like the perfect fit. It's a lovely place, and nothing like Yarmouth, which is full of smackheads and teenage girls with pushchairs. That's a dump, and well known for it. After I went there I said to Karen: "I wouldn't mind coming down here." We started looking about, and I came across a beautiful listed house. It had six bedrooms over four floors and lovely old gardens. The garage even had a pit in it, so you could go under your car.

The owner was a lovely old girl called Mrs Rose, who still dressed like it was the 1920s. She might have been in her 90s, but she was still sharp. When she showed us the house she was wearing a hat with a little flap on the side that made her look like Elmer J. Fudd from *Looney Tunes*. When she said we could bring our Rottweiler, Bomber, I offered to take it straightaway and put in six months' rent, which was about £6,000. The house was lovely, but she'd inherited it and had never touched it. It looked like it had been frozen in the 1960s.

I clicked with Mrs Rose, and after we moved in she invited us round for a meal to her lovely 1930s house, which had its own tennis courts round the back. Mrs Rose was very wealthy, and had made a lot of money playing the stock markets. When we were there she took me into her garage and showed me her Morgan sports car – one of the first ones that ever came off the production line. She said she knew the owner of the Morgan factory. Before we had dinner, she went down into her cellar and brought up a box of champagne. It was from about 1830, and was so dusty even I didn't drink it. I didn't want to embarrass her, so I just pretended to sip it then spat it down the toilet.

I liked her. She had a bit of character about her. She used to go on a lot of cruises where she'd always have dinner with the captain. Her husband had died, but was very wealthy too. He was involved in shipping.

I carried on selling cars there, specialising in Mercedes. The double garage and pit made me look more professional, and I was doing all right. But that didn't make things any easier with Karen. Our problems only got worse down there. We were getting on the gear quite heavily. It was getting back to like before.

There was a bit of a party scene. I wasn't going out, but we were having a lot of late nights indoors. She started going to a gym again so I knew something was up. I put the kids in a local school very briefly, but I took them out after they had a bit of grief from another kid with special needs. They were with me, selling cars and mooching about. Just like I was when I was a kid with my own father. We'd often go to Lowestoft for the day and see what's what.

All through this time, me and Karen kept drifting apart. It was a bad time, and that just made me get more on the gear and drink. I fucking caned it down there, and it was too much. I was binge-drinking four nights a week. I never used to get drunk, because I was taking coke at the same time. When you get drunk you have another line and bang, it brings you back up. When you're drunk you lounge about. That never happened to me. Regularly I was up until 7am. Eventually you just peter out and flatline because you're so fucked. You can't physically take any more gear because your body has shut down.

It went on like this for months. All the time, me and Karen were living on tenterhooks. It had got so rough that my sister came round to try and patch things up. She was a bit worried about me. She came round with her husband Ian (who later committed suicide over the gear). She asked me if I was going to make things up with Karen, even though she wasn't her biggest fan, truth be told. We were still living together, but it wasn't going well. The kids were suffering, as they always do in a bad marriage. Things were going up and down and I was shoving shit up my nose, not knowing what day it is. It isn't a nice experience for anyone. After a blazing row we'd often sit down and have a drink to try and patch things up. We'd have a couple of lines and be all lovey-dovey. It makes you want to get close together. But that soon wears off, and you can very quickly have an argument.

It can turn nasty very quickly. "What's your fucking problem?" I'd say. I never got violent towards her, but we had our fair share of heated rows. I used to tell her "Don't take me for a fucking mug. Tell me where you're going all day." I was no fool, and I knew something was up. She would go out to the gym every morning, and you just get that feeling that something isn't right. You just know it. You touch them, and they're a bit off. They're always bickering with you. .

We were falling out of love, which is a terrible time for anyone. You compensate for that by shoving a load of shit up your nose, thinking you're going to have unbelievable pornographic sex. You will have that a few times, and then it unwinds and you take another step back because the drug kicks in. Your sexual desires and your sexual antics go through the roof on cocaine.

You could be in a cupboard dressed as a traffic warden, but if that floats your boat then that's it. But once you get back to normal again the come-down is unbelievable. In the long run, all it does is make you drift further apart.

It got to the point when I couldn't even look at her. She was always hiding her phone, which just made me even more paranoid. I started looking at it because she made me suspicious. The drink and the gear makes you think she's hiding even more. Coke is a thinker's drug, and it makes you paranoid. I've always been a deep thinker anyway. When I was on coke I'd go to bed with a calculator in my head, thinking of every eventuality.

When the phone went off you'd say, "Who's that?" "Oh, someone rang the wrong number," she'd reply. That was bollocks and I knew something was going on, but when you're in love you lie to yourself. You push it under the carpet and have another line of coke to replace that reality check. When you're taking coke you don't live in the real world. It takes your problems and they disappear. You live in this fantasy world off your fucking nut. Nothing matters apart from the next line, having a drink, having a laugh and a joke. You'd ring up your mates that aren't your mates, and talk bollocks. That went on for quite a while, and it was a bad experience. We were there for 18 months in all. For most of the time I was so off my head I didn't know what day it was.

I still had a bit of cash left over and I was still selling cars, so I had enough money to survive. At one point, I nearly opened a shop in Gorleston. It used to be a butcher's, and I was going to turn it into a fishmonger's. I saw a gap in the market, but the idea quickly fell out of bed. The bloke who owned the shop was keen to start with, but then pulled the plug so it never went forward.

As it dawned on me that there was no prospect of opening a business in Gorleston, I thought about moving. It hadn't been the place I imagined. The move hadn't fixed my relationship, and after 18 months it was breaking down very badly. I know she was fucking around with someone. She said she was going to the gym every morning and night. I wasn't going to jump of Tower Bridge over it, but it was hurtful. I knew and – worse – my kids knew. I turned to drink and drugs to guard myself against it, and my cocaine habit became horrific by the end. I'd binge on Friday night and Saturday night. I'd get off the fucking Richter scale. I wasn't in control.

My cocaine addiction was getting to the point where I needed more and more to get that buzz. I was spending £500 on a Friday night alone. That was between me and her, and maybe someone else. We were doing that four times a week. I was going through the champagne, vodka, and wine too. We had these massive glasses you could fit half a bottle of wine in. Along with that I had tall tumblers that I'd drink vodka lemonade in. I washed all that down with a mountain of cocaine, which is a terrible cocktail. You get a headache from the vodka, the coke makes you buzz off your tits, and the wine makes you pissed.

While I was there, I started smoking too. I've never been one for fags, but sometimes I was smoking 60 a night. I would smoke one after another, just to distract me. It was fucking mental. I remember sitting there smoking fag butts when I ran out of cigarettes.

Nearly all the money I made off selling cars went on feeding my addictions. There's nothing wrong with spending money, but shoving it up your nose makes you a prize mug. I only learned that 30 years later.

After one heavy three-day binge I said, "Fuck it, we're moving." It was my defence mechanism against reality. She wasn't happy about that at all but reluctantly agreed. I need to get away from the horrific memories I had there.

Gorleston: apart from being out of my head, all I can remember is misery.

CHAPTER 18

—

NEWMARKET

We left Gorleston in a hurry because I was so determined to get out of there. We didn't even have enough time to find another place to rent, so as a temporary measure we stayed at my sister's house in Hockley, Essex, for about a month. I put all my stuff in storage because I wasn't sure where we were moving to. It was still a rough time, and got even worse when my sister saw me out of my head. She had loads of kids, and they saw it too. Her husband used to like the drink and the powder, which was a dreadful fucking scenario. Things got a bit heated. She used to come down in the morning, and we'd still be up, coked off our heads, sitting at the kitchen table. It's embarrassing, looking back. Julie has never taken any drugs. She wouldn't touch cocaine, especially after she's seen the state of me. She'd have an occasional drink but, unlike me, she knows when to call it a day.

There wasn't much to do in Essex apart from get out of my nut, so I'd pass most days looking for a new gaf. I didn't want to stay in Essex after my experience at West Mersea, and Norfolk and Suffolk were crossed off the list too. The next logical option was Cambridgeshire.

I'd always fancied myself as a bit of a racecourse-goer, so I picked Newmarket. It was new surroundings and new opportunities, I thought. We moved to a beautiful four-storey town house in a development called The Gallops, which cost £1,200 a month. We had to wait three weeks while everything was going through, so we stayed in a hotel called the Bedford Lodge. It's very well-known with all the horse people and jockeys, and was terrible for drink and drugs. It's got a health club and spa, and you could see the horses going down The Gallops when they were training.

I've always been into my fashion, and used to like dressing to impress. When I moved there I noticed that my fashion sense was out of sync with most people round there. They all used to wear long coats with felt collars, whereas I was sporting designer labels they wouldn't be seen dead in. To remedy that I visited a clothes shop called Golding in the High Street. I went in there looking like a fucking rapper and came out looking like Lester Piggott. I spent £3,000 on two coats with felt collars, a pair of nice slacks, a checkered shirt, a cravat, and a pairs of R M Williams boots. I wanted to buy two pairs but the bloke went, "I've only got one. We've got about ten pairs out there, but they're all sold to Sheik Mohammed bin Rashid Al Maktoum." He's the ruler of Dubai, and is big into racing. He apparently fell in love with Newmarket racecourse after visiting it while studying at Cambridge University in the 1960s. He owned a huge red-brick building at the top of the hill called Warren Towers. I never saw him personally, but he had bodyguards watching the place. It was like fucking Fort Knox.

After buying all my clobber I returned to the Bedford Lodge, dressed to the nines, thinking I was a racecourse man. Both me and Karen got heavily on the drink that night, and met this bloke who'd come down for the races. He made out he was the biggest gangster in the world and knew everyone. What a load of old rubbish. He started doing a bit of coke with me and Karen. We were buying champagne and having a good time. Around 2am he suddenly disappeared after we had a few words. He started saying things about gangsters, so I told him to fuck off. He left in a hurry and put the champagne on my bill, the cheeky fucker.

Living in a hotel was OK for a few days, but the novelty soon wore off and I was anxious to get into the house. The landlord was called Robert and he was a bit of a sap, who kept dragging his heels. In the end, I put my foot down and he gave us the keys.

It was relief being in the house. My mind was put at rest, and I set about planning my next business venture. I had an idea about setting up a luxury chauffeuring firm, taking punters from London to the races at the weekend. To do that I bought myself an S-class Mercedes 500 off a dealer at the Newmarket Motoring Company for £8,000. Originally it had belonged to the Dubai embassy, and it had bulletproof glass.

I called the business VIP Chauffeuring Service, and it was supposed to be a luxury taxi service complete with champagne. I had a couple of clients and didn't do too bad to start with. It could have taken off, but once again I got in with the wrong crowd of people and was doing too much gear. One guy I got friendly with was a trainer called David. He died from drinking too much. The worst thing was that no one was that shocked when it happened. It seemed to be one of those things that people just accepted around there.

That wasn't an isolated incident and I would say that Newmarket is, without doubt, the worst place for drink and drugs I've ever been. Every person down there seemed to be bang on the powder and bang on the drink. All those stable lads are working first thing in the morning, but they're finished by midday so they head straight to the pub. It's the same thing with jockeys. Many times I've seen big-name jockeys like Frankie Dettori in The Bedford Lodge having a drink. I followed suit and every day I'd be drinking vodka, wine and champagne down the bar. I'd be sniffing gear in the toilets, and meeting people who were into the same scene. It was never going to end well.

One couple we got friendly with were called John and Gloria. John used to work for the Godolphin stables, which is owned by Sheikh Mohammed and has some of the best racehorses in the world. He was bang on the powder, and didn't mind a drink either. The first night they came round the house we were on the landing and he said, "Can you get any gear?" Straightaway I got some off someone I'd met in the bar a few weeks earlier. That night turned into a messy one, and those sessions quickly became a weekly occurrence. They'd often end up spending more of their weekends round our house rather than theirs. John didn't know when to stop, and I forget the number of times he passed out on my floor, completely off his head. Gloria was no better, and she'd fall asleep when she couldn't take any more.

We'd often venture out into Cambridge, which is only down the road from Newmarket. I used to spend a lot of time down there at Michael Caine's restaurant, completely off my nut. I had the barman squared up after I gave him a couple of lines in the toilet. He was giving me cocktails for £1 a pop, normally they were £30. He was so out of his nut that he didn't care. After he'd had a couple of lines he had a bad turn and stood in the corner scowling. I took him back in the toilet, gave him another couple of lines and he livened up. He was serving people double-time after that.

We were in there one night when I got talking to a bloke who owned a company called Speedy Tool Hire. He turned to be a bit of prick, and was another one who got on the coke. He got a little bit abrupt, and I had to pull him up. I took him outside, and he got his stuff and fucked off. He was throwing his weight around, saying this and that, but he didn't buy a drink. He was coming on to my old lady, she loved all that of course, but it didn't go down too well with me. I even took my two sons up there, and one of my sister's daughters. She said to me recently, "I remember you spending £1,800 in there on a big meal." I didn't eat it, just pushed it around the table, because I was so out of it. The kids had a meal, and loads of drinks. After that I went into the bar and bought everyone a drink. I ended up talking to a Canadian couple, who both kissed me. It was just one of those nights.

After a long night drinking down Cambridge or the Bedford Lodge we'd head back to our house and carry on until the early hours. It was like West Mersea all over again. We realised that, and vowed to calm down. But we barely lasted a day most times. I was surrounded by people who were using, and that's not the best environment to get clean in. My relationship with Karen remained on the rocks. Like before, she quickly joined a gym and was going missing a lot. The kids briefly went to school, but I pulled them out after we had a bit of trouble. After that they spent most of their time with me. We'd stay indoors or go out to a café in Newmarket that was run by a couple called Tom and Fran that I got to know well. I carried on selling cars and ticking over, but I craved another business.

In my mind I struggled to find a purpose, and was deeply unhappy with the way things were going. With very little to do I started going on aimless drives around the countryside. On one of these I visited a small town called Haverhill that is just over the border from Cambridgeshire, in Suffolk. Mooching around there, I spotted a shop with an office going for £70 a week. It was in the middle of a bunch of houses and had a private landlord, so was right up my street. I had this crazy idea that I thought might make money and save my relationship with Karen at the same time.

We were still just hanging in there at this point, and I reckoned this business could bring us back from the brink. I said to her: "Why don't we open up a model and promotion agency?" She agreed, and we created Faces Modelling and Promotion

Agency. From the word go it caused fucking uproar in Haverhill. They hated me in that town, but I didn't care. We signed up anyone who came in as long as they paid £195. Karen tried to look professional by vaguely working the computer. We boarded off the back of it and had a photographic studio. I bought a camera for £150 and started taking photographs of people.

They weren't going to win any Pulitzers, but then the subjects weren't exactly oil paintings either.

After we took the photos, we punted them round trying to get work for models. It worked on a few occasions. I remember we got a photoshoot for a company called Bear. They were the biggest Harley Davidson dealer in Britain. I went up there with three girls, scantily dressed of course. I took a lot of pleasure in taking those photos.

Try as I might I wasn't David Bailey, but we had a stroke of luck when a fella walked into the shop and said he was a photographer. His name was Andrew, and he'd done a bit of work for *Max Power* magazine. He was a right fucking geek, but a great photographer. He said, "Why don't we start working together?" I agreed, and we set about promoting the business. Like with all my other ventures, I made sure that everyone in that town heard about my photography business. And it worked. I was getting people coming in straightaway. Half the town signed up in the end, and we were taking good money. They're a strange bunch down there. It's a very small gene pool, if you ask me. A lot of them came in and said, "I want to be a model." They might look like the Elephant Man but I'm not going to say no, am I? As long as they paid £195 and were over 18 there were no issues. I had all the right forms, so it was all legal. We soon branched out, and Karen started doing kids and baby modelling. It was very successful, and we had loads of parents coming in. Who doesn't want their kid to be a model? They'd say, "She's a model." Really, she looks like a horror story, but as long as they pay their £195 it's fine.

With the business ticking over, Andrew suggested we started doing portfolios for people. We charged people £395 for 12 pictures that we'd lay out nicely in a book. Next door to the shop there was a community centre. I got it squared up with the fella to rent the hall out for £30 an hour. I used to give the photographer £150, so I'd cop £225 for not much work. To avoid getting too much grief when people didn't get work, I said beforehand that I couldn't guarantee anything. A lot of them weren't going to go too far because they were ugly fuckers, but it was money at the end of the day. They could still show their portfolio to their boyfriend and family. The portfolios were really popular and we ended up having to stay up late putting them together quite often, which was a good sign.

Instead of leaving the business to tick over, my next great plan was to open an escort agency on the sly round the back. The minute I started putting ads out for it we had all sorts coming through the door. We had a lot of blokes ringing up to join and book clients. To my surprise, a lot of women called up wanting to book blokes as well. I was charging them £500 to come on the books. I wasn't guaranteeing them work, but I said there was a strong possibility. It worked a treat, and we had dozens of people sign up within days.

One geezer called Colin kept ringing up saying he wanted to come in. I said to Karen, "I can't cope with all these fucking pervs ringing up. They're driving me mad." Colin wouldn't give up though, so I told him to come round. I'd be on the gear when he walked in. He had an old black and white Adidas bag.

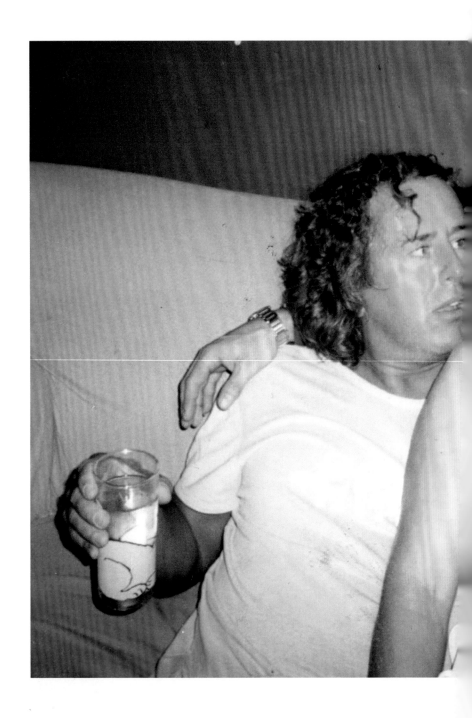

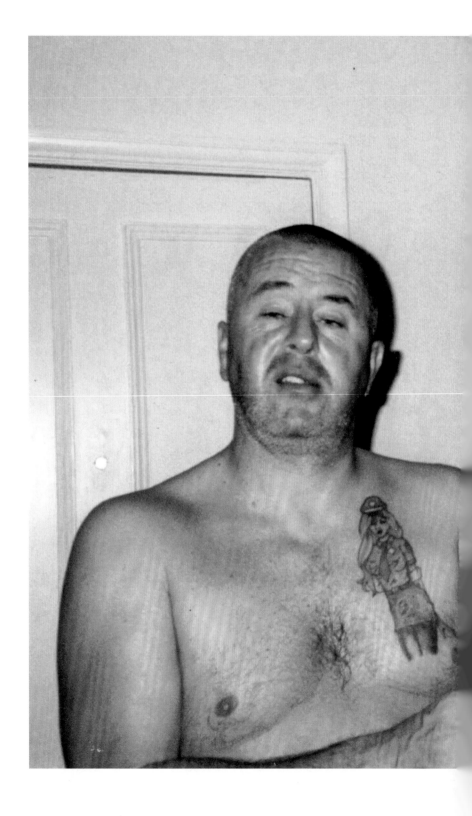

He was a big ginger lump who looked like a scaffolder. Even though I was fucked I thought, "What's he got that bag for?" He said, "I want to get changed into my gear", so he went out the back. I was taking the pictures for the escort agency because I wanted to keep it under wraps. He was 15 minutes and I was thinking "What the fuck is he doing?"

When he came back out he was totally dressed as a woman, complete with stockings and suspenders. I was in bits, and couldn't look at him. Before we got going I had a couple of lines just to gather myself. When we were doing the pictures, he was bending over and showing everything. I took the £500 off him but I don't think he ever got much work out of it. When he left I couldn't stop laughing. That was one of the funniest experiences of my life. That night I got completely off my head: it was a culture shock to me. I'd heard about people doing that sort of thing, but never experienced it first-hand.

For the next year the business ticked over nicely. The escort agency was steady, and we were giving the escorts a 70/30 per cent split. I was promoting it with little £15 box ads in the *Haverhill Echo*, which all the town's perverts seemed to read. Whenever we had a booking I'd drive the escorts to the venue and make sure they were OK. Having tried my hand at escorting I went one step further and set up a strippergram agency. We had quite a few people sign up, and bookings were coming. I did quite a few stag and hen nights, which were nice earners. But as soon as it got established people twigged that it was linked to the modelling company. That threw a spanner in the works, and proved to be my undoing.

All of a sudden people stopped coming in to sign up for the modelling agency, because they'd heard it was an escort agency.

One and one is two, and all of a sudden you're accused of running an illegal brasshouse. It wasn't, but that's what people thought, which was enough to put them off. It was all legal, but people don't like any association with strippers or escorts. At the same time so-called models were coming in and moaning because they weren't getting any work. All the while I was using coke and drinking. Things started to slip and we weren't opening on time, or at all. That pissed people off even more and put off potential customers. The business had temporarily revived my marriage and we had a brief few months where we enjoyed working together chasing the pound note. But as things fell apart so did we, and things were rapidly fizzling away.

The worse things got, the more gear I took. I was taking every day and would do heavy sessions at the weekends with Karl and Marion. At weekends we get through at least £1,800 between the four of us. I'd wake up on Monday morning feeling fucked, and have a little livener to get me going. I might struggle through Tuesday with only half a gram, but as soon as some money came in I'd be back heavily on the powder. What used to do it for me was one glass of wine. After a couple of sips, I'd be up saying "Right, let's go." But I could never have one line of coke. No one on this planet can have one line, because it grabs hold of you. I was drinking a hell of a lot of Le Montrachet wine there. It was good stuff, but you'd expect that for £35 a bottle. I'd easily drink three or four bottles of it in an evening. Sometimes I'd mix it up and have a bottle of Smirnoff, six grams of coke and a bottle of wine. Imagine that: when you crash you're fucked, and in a bad way. Your heart is beating, and you're all over the place.

I shut the office down when people started deserting the business. People started making a few complaints so I thought,

"Fuck it, it's time to ping." No one got any money back because the business was finished. I'd say, "You've been here, you signed up, you didn't get any work, that's tough." It was a bit blunt, but that's the way it goes sometimes. It was a blessing in disguise, because I could barely cope anyway.

Things get messy when you're up until 7am coked out of your mind. You don't know what day it is, and can barely remember your own name. It was going on a regular basis, and I was spending all the money I earned on gear and booze. I was making about £4,000 a week, it was never in the same league as the pine and it wasn't going to get me a Coutts bank account, but it was enough to feed my habits.

After that I carried on selling cars to keep my head above water. Obviously, I was still using a considerable amount of cocaine and not really realising what was going on. The relationship was hanging on by a very small thread. We were bickering a lot about stupid little things. It used to go on and on. Whenever things came to a head we'd say, "We're getting off the gear, we're not doing it no more, our lives are spiralling out of control." At the time we meant it, but the next day you do it again. It was always "Let's start a fresh one tomorrow," but it never happened. My addiction had got to the stage where I always made a point of having it on me. In the early stage of my addiction I never really put myself out to get coke. If it was there I'd have some, but if it wasn't then fine. By that time, when I knew I really had a problem, I panicked on the odd occasion I didn't have any. For insurance, I made sure I had a couple of dealers' numbers to hand so a ready supply was only a phone call away.

I always did my best to look presentable. I still had all my racing clobber, and always made a point of going out looking the bollocks. A lot of cocaine addicts are tramps, but I always used to be smart and make sure I went on the sun bed. But I couldn't hide the fact that I was very overweight. I'd put a lot of weight on in West Mersea, but that ballooned even more in Newmarket. People say coke-heads can't get fat but that's bollocks, you can go either way. After a two-day binge, when you've eaten nothing, all you want to do is scoff yourself. You eat anything and everything, from pizzas to ice cream, and wash it down with lattés and pop. That lifestyle meant I went up to about 17 stone, which for a man of my size was ridiculous. I ended up looking like a fat Les Dawson. As a young man I was always about 12 stone, but with the drugs, the drink and the binge food it came on very quickly.

I never did any exercise whatsoever. By the time I'd been in Newmarket a year I had a beer belly, a double chin, and was terribly out of condition. I was in a fucking dreadful state. That was the effects of the drink. It got out of control in Newmarket. When I went to Haverhill it got even worse, until I was drinking every night. I even bought these special wine glasses from Ley and Wheeler. They were very big, two glasses and a bottle is gone. I remember people used to say, "Don't go round his house, he'll give you a bottle of wine and you're fucked." They were like a bowl, and they were dear.

Eventually at The Gallops it got to a stage where it was a party house. People were coming round on a regular basis until the early hours. We'd start off in the Bedford Lodge with the kids and go back to the house, where we'd get out of our heads. It wasn't a nice experience for anyone, especially the kids. The chauffeuring business never really materialised, and I sold the car for £5,000. When the modelling agency collapsed I knew it was time to move on. The rent was a bit late one month not because we didn't have it but because we were drunk or coked-up. I had a few words with him, as you do, and he gave us two months' notice and asked us to leave.

CHAPTER 19

—

EXNING, SUFFOLK

Our next house was a big bungalow about a hundred yards from Frankie Dettori's mansion. I carried on selling cars, but I wasn't doing a lot else apart from getting high. It was getting to a bad point in our relationship. Karen was still going to the gym and missing for hours on end. It still wasn't right, and it hadn't been for a long time.

We were using so much that we started drifting apart. Coke does that to you. You tend to have these unbelievable sexual desires followed by a wild night of sexual activity. The next day you wake up and it's all gone. You feel cold. It's hard to explain, but it's not a nice feeling. We were there for less than six months before we moved on.

While I was out in Newmarket I mentioned about moving somewhere new. It was then that someone mentioned a house they knew that was up for rent in Exning, a nice little village in Suffolk. It was a four-bedroom semi going for £950 a month. I went down there and liked the look of it. The next-door neighbour was even all right. He used to modify little VW vans and sell them on. We moved in, and I immediately started selling cars. Business was steady and I started to feel better, like I had more purpose to my life. I never stopped taking drugs or drinking, but in these brief spells things would quieten down. Like before, though it wasn't to last, and quickly my demons came back to haunt me. I should have cut all ties with Newmarket, but I made a fatal error when we started going back to the Bedford Lodge on a regular basis. We had a few messy ones in there, and that spilled over back to the new house. Within weeks it was back to the party scene and late nights. We were going to the Bedford Lodge so much that we were getting invited round to these horse trainers' houses for parties.

Every party we went to, everyone was on the gear. It was a very extreme area for coke, and compares to London. Racecourse people are party people. When we were in that house I got involved with some people down there. I was still having problems with Karen. The kids were a little bit older now. They were never trouble, but they could tell what was going on. We were in that house for about eight months.

I had a little bit of a problem with a horse trainer called Robert. He was the ex-husband of Fran, the woman who had the cafe in Newmarket. They were doing some dodgy pyramid sales scheme. We met up in the Bedford Lodge one night and he came round my house afterwards, where we got on the powder. I gave him a Louis Vuitton sunglasses case which I'd bought in Venice years earlier. He seemed grateful, and everything seemed fine with his life. But a couple of days later I heard that he'd been going round telling people I was a drug dealer. I went down to his stables to find him, and got him in the back of my Mercedes E-class with one of my mates. Before I could say anything, he physically pissed himself in my car. I said, "Why have you been talking shit about me? I invited you round my house and let you sniff my gear. I even gave you a sunglasses case, and you go around saying I'm a drug dealer." He didn't say a word, and ran off the second he could.

For all my sins, I've never been a drug dealer. I admit I was buying it, but I wasn't selling it. It really gives me the hump when people talk shit about me, and I'm not the sort of person to take it lying down.

That minor skirmish led to me falling out with a few people down there. It wasn't anything major, and I was never too worried, but it gave me a good excuse to pull out of there and find somewhere else.

Around this time, one of Julie's sons came down to live in the area. He got into a little bit of trouble back in Essex, so I took him under my wing. He was only in his 20s and I brought him on the firm so to speak. He used to come round on a regular basis to drink. He met a girl down there who he ended up staying with for a while. He spent a lot of time with me as a kid, so he looked up to me. That's what he told me, anyway. He was involved with me, selling cars, and used to help me do them up before I flogged them on.

While we were living in Exning, I was driving into Ely one day when I saw a yard for rent. I thought it might make a decent car wash because it was right next to the station. It used to belong to a Willhire van hire company, which was like Hertz. There was a sign and an office and a big yard to rent with an acre of land. Next door was an engineering factory. It turned out that the bloke who ran the factory owned the site. His name was John, and we quickly struck up a friendship. I took that yard and very quickly thought I'd turn it into a car park and a car wash. There were no spaces in the station car park every morning, so I thought it would be easy money.

It was a big mistake, and it fucking bombed. I had a concrete slab laid, bought all the car wash equipment and a valeting centre, which wasn't cheap. What I didn't initially think of was the level crossing. The gates used to go down, and that really fucked me up. People used to come out of there, and if the gates were down they couldn't get out. At busy times, they'd stay closed for 20 minutes. After a day's work people just wanted to get home, so most people would go and park elsewhere. That said, it was still making a bit of money, because I only charged £5 a day to park and £10 for a wash. I employed two kids there called Jimmy and another lad Simon, a funny lad who used to be in borstal. I did have a few good days there. It used to be full up and most people who leave me their keys for the valeting. I think it was £35 for a full valet. But it wasn't as successful as I thought it would be.

As well as selling cars, I started selling vans. That's when I fell out with John and it all went tits-up. We were really friendly at first. We used to wash all the cars he was selling. But he got a little bit saucy to me one day. To cut to the chase, he said, "You can't sell vans here." I told him where to go, and he never spoke to me after that. It was a shame because we were doing very well, especially selling minibuses. I used to go to the British Car Auction, there was one in King's Lynn, and buy a few of them. I'd get British Leyland ones in, really cheap, for about £1,200. I was valeting them inside and out and getting a mechanic I had working for me to give them a once-over. He was a little mobile mechanic who came in there one day in a van. He was a little grease monkey, but he was good at his job. I didn't pay him much, but he seemed more than happy to do the work. After he'd looked at them I'd flog them on for £3,000. A lot of scout troops, community centres and churches used to come and buy them. They couldn't afford new ones, so they were over the moon when I sold them a cut-price one. We also started renting out old bangers for £100 a week. We were selling a lot of convertibles there too, like Peugeot 205s and Fort Escorts. Things started picking up there.

I was there for about a year, but things weren't good indoors. I was still drinking, and it increased when I started pulling in £4,000 a week. But I was still going through a terrible patch with her. We had a distant relationship. I was drinking heavily, and bingeing. We had a lot of late nights and I still knew a lot of people from Newmarket. It was only down the road. My coke consumption hadn't gone down, so I wasn't on point.

At the time you don't realise it, but it affects the business and your mental attitude, and slowly things start to slip away from you. You're increasing your drinking and coke use to try and hide the reality that you're losing the business and losing your family. I was only there about a year, but things slipped away very quickly. It's a shame, because the business had a lot of potential. As things got worse at home, I started turning up later. I'd let the two young kids open up. I was even doing gear in the office there. I can even remember a geezer who used to pull up in a black Mercedes CL coupe. He was a trader in the city. He mentioned something to me one day, and I ended up doing a bit of coke with him one day. After that he came in on a regular basis, him and his mate. He was an older man, but very wealthy and smart.

Once again, wherever I went I ended up getting involved with people who take the drug. Talking bollocks again, as you do when you're on the powder. Things slowly but surely spiralled out of control, but I just kept on using. The relationship was at a very bad point. We were talking, but there wasn't a lot of love there. Things were like a yo-yo, constantly up and down. One minute you're all right, the next you're at each other's throats. Even without the gear it wasn't right. The feelings weren't right. It was slowly deteriorating. I saw it coming. You do what you can to keep things going. But when you have a problem and you're using you take a bit more coke and drink a bit more to hide the reality of real life, and that's a terrible thing. The kids used to see us rowing, shouting, which wasn't nice for them. They'd come down the stairs at 4am and see us up, coked off our tits. They went to school on and off while we were living there, but it was never anything permanent.

CHAPTER 20

—

CLACTON

It was back to Essex as I tried to save my marriage again by moving. This time we rocked up at Clacton-on-Sea. The first house we rented was just outside the town, and had a right weird landlord called Sandra. She was one of these Greenpeace people who was constantly smoking roll-ups. It was a lovely three-bed place, but hadn't been touched in years. She'd inherited it off her dad, and it was in probate while they sold his estate off. She said she just wanted someone in for a few months before it was sold. I just needed something short-term, so I was happy with that.

Right from the off I had the feeling that something wasn't right about her. We moved in a couple of days after I gave her £850 for the deposit and a month's rent. When we moved in I realised how out-of-date it all was. All her dead dad's stuff was in there, like the carpets and furniture. The furniture was like it was made in the 1700s. From the moment we moved in, she went all weird on us. After four days, she said, "I haven't had any references from you." I told her she never asked for any. She insisted she did and said she wanted us out. When I refused, she brought her brother round and got really funny.

Now I realise she was trying to con the deposit out of us. When they started getting a bit fresh I said, "Bollocks, I'm not moving out of here." Her brother, who was a tall, skinny geezer, came round when Martin and Albert were there at the time. I was out, and Karen was probably down the gym. They started banging on the window saying, "Let us in." The boys rang me and I turned up in my little Transit van. I said, "What are you doing?" She said, "I want you out tonight." I had a terrible row with the pair of them. Eventually I said fuck this and went indoors. I came back out with a baseball bat, which I always have in the house.

They left after that.

I said to Karen, "We've got to get out of this place, something isn't right." Luckily, I found another house round the corner that was available immediately. I rang up this woman, Margaret, and said, "I want my money back." I'd only been there four days. When she refused I said, "If I don't get my money back I'm going to smash the place to pieces and cause £10,000 worth of damage. Do what you like." The agreement was, on the day that I move I give her the keys back there and then. I never let her in before. On the day, she came round and said, "You aren't getting anything." She was with her brother again. So I went to the van and got the baseball bat. I said to her brother, "This is going right across your head, mate." She had the money in her pocket and gave it to me.

After that we moved to Clacton-on-Sea. I rented a bungalow off a bloke who was an absolute lunatic. He had a lot of property in the area. He was fucking filthy, and the house wasn't much better. It was a four-bed bungalow with a massive garden with fishponds in it. It wasn't badly kitted out, but the toilet and kitchen were dreadful.

After the mess in the previous house, I thought I'd better get back to making money. I'd been in a bad place with the gear and booze for a while so I decided to open a new business. I found two shops to rent, and went back into furniture. One was in Kirby near Frinton-on-Sea, and the other was in Clacton. Frinton is one of the poshest places in Essex. It's the only place in Essex where they wouldn't allow pubs until recently. There are no cafes. Someone was selling ice creams on the sea front and they stopped him.

The other one was in Old Road, Clacton, next to Morrison's and a sauna parlour. I drove by there and saw a To Let sign handwritten in the window. I rang it up and met Edith, the landlady. She was a switched-on woman from a family who were very big sweet manufacturers. Her grandfather had been in the chocolate business in the 1920s and had owned that shop for years. It was fucking massive, and had an upstairs and a big bit at the back. I thought it was going to be great. It was only £100 a week. I called it Seconds Out – after one of my shops in Leyton.

I very quickly started making money there. Clacton is a strange area. It's not the richest place, but they don't mind spending money. Even in the poorer areas like Jaywick – AKA Benefits On Sea – they're the same. If they've got £100 they'll spend £90 on a bed. So I thought, I'll do a bit of pine, mainly cheap tables and chairs. I sold them for £199, single beds cost £69, double beds were £99 and I did some budget beds for £89. They were shit, but it flew off the shelf. I was there about six weeks and it took off. I was taking good money, and on an average week it would be around £5,000.

By the late 2000s solid pine was so popular. To make even more money I focused on second-hand stuff. I used to buy decent stuff, not the old shit you see in a lot of places. I used to go to an auction house in Colchester called Remus and Dempsey, and buy a lot of chaise longues. The profit is unbelievable in second-hand furniture. House clearances were a good money-earner, too. I used to put a little ad in the paper and say 'Three-piece suites wanted'. I would buy a suite for £40, clean and sell it for £350. You wouldn't believe the amount of suites I got off old people. I wasn't ripping them off, because they just wanted rid of it. I'd go round in my van, give them a few quid, clean it up and sell it on. It got so busy that people were coming up to me before I even got it off the van.

Eventually I started doing a bit of solid pine, after I'd waxed it upstairs. The trade was just on its last legs and starting to go out of fashion, but people were still buying it. The shop had a one-bedroom flat upstairs which I turned into a studio. I turned the bedroom into a waxing room and had an ex-con I knew called Paul Finch working in there (I'll tell you more about him later).

I opened the second shop in Kirby in 2008, about seven months after the first one. I saw it for rent and thought I'd go for it. It had a forecourt and a flat. I took the whole lot. I put my nephew in there, who was later on to cause me a lot of trouble. I met the landlord, who was a very wealthy man, and he let me have it for £800 a month. The flat had been redone and was brand new. I agreed with my nephew that he could go into the flat with his bird and we'd run the shop together. He paid the rent on the flat, ran the shop and we went 50/50 on the £800 rent, plus we'd split the profits from the shop.

It was a great deal and could have been a cash cow, but he fucked it up. He didn't have his heart in it. He wasn't opening up on time, and the shop was run down. I'd go down there and the furniture wouldn't be ready. He wasn't on my level. He was drinking, and arguing with his partner. He couldn't cope doing both at the time, so things seized up. I did make money out of it eventually, but he wasn't firing on all cylinders. After five months, I said, "bollocks you can completely take the shop off me." I thought, "There's no light at the end of the tunnel here. This is a fucking dead duck. He isn't going to pull his socks up." He was there for another seven months by himself before it folded.

After about a year with the filthy landlord, things came to a head. The bungalow had terrible damp, and when I asked him to sort it out he refused. I had intentions of moving anyway because it wasn't exactly a palace, but I was still spending good money on rent and he should have fixed any problems. He came round and got a bit fresh, and I told him to stick his house up his arse. He didn't do any repairs because he was so tight. I said "I'm coming out of here soon," and he was fine with that.

I was doing a delivery in Harwich, which was just outside Clacton, when I spotted my next house. It was an 11-bedrom mansion on Marine Parade. From the moment I saw it I thought, "That's a lovely place." It was a four-storey Victorian Italian-style house that used to be a hotel, and would have been stunning when it was built. It had five bathrooms, and every bedroom had an en-suite. Everything was original, and it was furnished to a high spec. It still had the original windows, but because of the sea salt it needed a lot of work. In my bedroom, you opened one door and it went into an office. Another door led you onto a balcony four times bigger than most people's sitting rooms. The sea is 20ft away.

I went past there recently, and my furniture is still out on the decking. I'd be surprised if anyone's been in there since I left nearly 10 years ago. It needed a lot of work and most people would want to update it, but it was my kind of style. I liked the mosaic walls and all the coving. The carpets were plain. The rooms had very high ceilings with coving. It had double skirting. Every room had an open fire in. It was like something out of an Italian film. All the walls were plastered and had marble in. It had encrusted wallpaper with pictures of women on crowns. In the kitchen there was a huge Aga oven. It even had a little square board with bells on for the servants. At the back of the kitchen there was a stairwell that led down to a wine cellar. I filled it up with £3,000 of Cristal, and as always I said it was an investment. That plan lasted about five minutes, because I drank it all. When we were there I was always running down to the cellar. It was quite funny: we'd say,

"We'll only have one bottle." In reality, it was one after the other. If I was rich I would have stayed there for the rest of my life. It was fucking unbelievable.

It was owned by this head-case solicitor called Felicity who ran a practice in Clacton. She'd been left it in a will, and wanted to get rid of it. I made an inquiry and went to view it. When I went inside I instantly fell in love with it. At the time, I had an old-fashioned gold Mercedes 450SLC Sport, which is a very rare car. I spotted it sitting outside a flower shop run by a farmer in Weeley, just outside Clacton. When I spoke to him he said his wife had died of cancer. He bought it for her but she never got the chance to drive it. He said, "I don't really want to sell it, but when I see it in the garage it breaks my heart." I said, "Listen mate, how much do you want for it?" He said, "I can tell you're a genuine fella," so he sold it to me for £1,000. It was worth about £8,000. He just made me promise to look after it, which I did.

The rent was about £1,100 and we got it with an option to buy it for £350,000. That might sound cheap for an 11-bedroom house but, believe me, it was expensive for Harwich. It's a horrible town, with hardly anything there. There are no little shops, just chains. The only place it had that was any good was called the Pier Restaurant, which had the same owners as Le Talbooth in Colchester. It's very well known because it's got a fish restaurant upstairs and a grill downstairs. The fish restaurant is fully booked for three months because their food comes straight from the sea. It's a 30-second walk to the beach from there, so you know it's fresh. I was the best customer there. I got to know the head waiter well. He was called Nick.

Things were looking up when we moved into that house. My shop was going very well, and turning over £6,000 most weeks when we really got going. A lot of it was profit because I was buying second-hand stuff in cheap. When I started introducing the pine back, it really took off. I must have furnished about ten hotels down there. The first person who walked in owned a pub round the corner. I think he spent £8,000 cash. I put more pine out. Clacton is a very busy town. There are a lot of chimney pots and nosey neighbours. You'd have Mr and Mrs Jones buying some pine, so everyone would want one. I started selling sofas there too. Three-piece suites. I used to buy them for £225 and they'd go out for £559. Others I'd get in for £350 and sell them on for £750. It was good money all day long. There are loads of caravan parks in that area so I found a company that used to sell sofas which fitted through the small doors. I sold hundreds of them, and was making a good living. The caravan lot are odd, with their sovereign rings on, and slippers and socks, but they didn't mind spending some cash.

With money coming in I furnished that house from top to bottom. I bought everything at the Rams and Dempsey auction house in Colchester, including seven Chesterfield sofas. I put a green-button one with a matching captain's chair in my office. I had so many I even put one in my Martin's room. We had a table in there with 16 chairs. You'd need a megaphone to speak to the person at the other end in the dining room. The garden was in terraces on three different levels. At the very back there was a double garage. I had my dog at the time, and had a 30-foot square kennel for my Rottweiler Bomber to live in.

I enjoyed it there for the first three months. I was still drinking and doing gear, probably about four times a week, and I was still spending £500 a week on the stuff, but it wasn't at the previous levels. But like before, I started having problems with Karen again. She was a fucking nuisance, truth be told.

The kids didn't go to school, and instead they used to come out in two big vans we had. Karen was always hiding her phone when it was ringing. She was always doing tricks, like going to the toilet with her phone and going missing for hours. She started getting friendly with a couple of women who came into the shop, right old Clacton crackheads. It was bad news. That's when the partying started again. We were inviting undesirable people, round and it started getting out of control again.

We met most of them through the shop. One particular bloke came in who thought he was the bollocks, because he had a left-hand-drive Cadillac. We got chatting and said we'd go out for a meal. I took them to the Pier fish restaurant. He brought his old dolly bird with him. She might have had fake tits, but talk about mutton dressed as lamb. I showed him round the house first. Me and Karen had a bit of gear. His other half did too, but he abstained. After that we went into the Pier and drank Cristal champagne. They actually rang up Le Tolbooth because I was the only person who drank Cristal there and they had to order it in. We had a good drink, and spent £800. He was a bit slow coming forward with the cash, but at the time I just paid the bill. After that we went back to their house. It was there I learned what a weird pair they were.

They said they were swingers, and wanted to know if we fancied a go. She was a 4/10 normally, but when you've had a few grams of coke that becomes an 8/10. Your lust goes through the roof. It's off the Richter scale, so I was up for it. But it went all pear-shaped when he got a bit funny with Karen. He was getting touchy-feely, and she went mental because she was on the gear. After she told him to fuck off he got a bit fresh and I had to put him in his place. They both shit themselves and we left. A few weeks later I saw him in Clacton thinking he was the bollocks in his Cadillac. He was a bit shaky when I said, "You owe me £400, mate. Bring me the money over at 4pm, and don't be late." He was there on the dot. I wasn't in so he gave the money to Karen and fucked off.

That was the sort of people that came round. We tended to attract weirdoes. But at the time you don't see the bad in people, it's just party time. She used to have a few of her mates round too, as did I. One of my mates would come round and things frequently got out of control. Dyson was around a lot, and we'd often end up having fun.

Between the brief moments when we were all lovey-dovey, it quickly it became apparent we weren't getting on. She was going down the gym in Clacton a lot and getting very friendly with a woman called Lesley. She was a horrible woman with a big mouth. She thought she was the bollocks because her old man was in the nick for fraud. She used to come round a lot, sniffing gear. Not that she ever paid for it, so I had to foot the bill. I couldn't stand her. She instigated trouble, and tried to cause friction between me and Karen. Things slowly took a slide. Life was slipping away.

The more fractious things got at home, the more the business crumbled. I was still making money, but I started to have a lot of arguments. I had a lot of late nights. I was very heavy on the drink, especially the champagne and wine. Every week we'd spend four days partying on the coke and booze, and the other three recovering. The boys were getting older, and it was no way for them to live.

CHAPTER 21

—

THE PARTY

A few months after moving in we decided to have a party. I wasn't getting on with her at the time so we were on tenterhooks. I thought a good piss-up might clear the air. I invited a couple of mates and a few people from the local shops. One was an alcoholic barber called Ken. You wouldn't dare go into his shop at 1pm because he'd be shaking from all the booze. At 10am you were all right. After midday and he'd been in the pub for two hours he was like Shakin' Stevens so you'd better steer clear, especially if he got the cutthroat out. He'd take your head off.

We had about 16 people round including my aunt and my nephew with his then girlfriend and their baby daughter, who was only a few months old at this point. I booked a singer and this mixed-race geezer from Bethnel Green called Sly turned up. He was a good singer, and everyone was cracking away. I got about £1,000 of drink in, and a load of coke to make it a heavy session. It started in the garden at about 1pm. The singer was there in front of these massive speakers. I had food and an outside tent. It was like going to Monaco in Harwich. Everyone was drinking away, and taking plenty of coke on board. We were banging away with the music getting on with the gear and booze.

Then I get a knock on the door from this bloke who lived half a mile away. The nearest neighbour. He didn't say anything. He was a big guy, about 6ft 3, with glasses, and he got really fresh. I was very overweight at the time and totally fucked, but I've always been able to handle myself. I said, "Fuck off. It's one in the afternoon."

About an hour later we were drinking on the top level of the garden where I had a big patio. I saw the same bloke on top of my garage. He was throwing bricks over the garden wall.

One of them missed my nephew's baby by an inch. He went ballistic and jumped over the wall like a raving lunatic. I thought, this is bollocks. It was about 4pm. I was on the gear. We all jumped over the wall and he's squaring up to me. One thing led to another and I beat the fuck out of him in the middle of the street.

All the party people came out. The barber, and even the singer and DJ were involved. It was a bad fight. I was the only one really throwing any punches. The others did a lot of shouting, as they do. He went into one and squared up to me, and I hit him about three or four times. I broke his glasses. I then dragged him by the head across the road, and took him out the alleyway where the garage was. I told him politely to fuck off. He wasn't seriously injured at that point but he still came back at me again. His wife was screaming and shouting. He did physically attack me and threw bricks over our wall, so he deserved what he got.

I said, "You'd better go home, or you're going to get yourself seriously injured here." But he kept coming back. So the fight went on for a while. It went out into the road, and cars were stopping. He kept coming back at me. I think he hit me once or twice, but I hit him about 20 times. He was all over the place. Karen came out and had a row with his wife. She hit me in the face, so Karen pulled her back and her bra came off. When she hit me, I had no alternative but to retaliate. I knocked her 3ft in the air. She was spark out. That is the only time I have ever hit a woman in my life.

She was going mental, scratching me, pulling my hair and trying to bite me. I had him on me as well, so I've done the same with him. They were both on the floor, spark out. Two women in an office came down and said, "What's going on here?" They said they saw it all happen, and it wasn't my fault. They then came back to the party and got cracking. When it all went to court they gave evidence against me, the arseholes.

Eventually the couple went, because they were in trouble. They got themselves together and scampered down the road. They'd had a hiding. It was then back to the party, which went on until 4am. Everyone was taking massive amounts of gear. The singer said, "I've got to go at 8pm, to another venue." I gave him £500 to stay. He was off his fucking nut at the end of it. His singing got worse and worse. He started off like Barry White, by the end of it he was Tom White from down the road.

The barber was a bit of a character. When that fight was going on he scraped his hand down the wall and made out he was involved. My son saw him. I said, you never threw a punch. He was a Freemason. I never instigated it, but I threw the punches. It was like a pub brawl. There's not many people who will really fight. That's what happened in court: they said I instigated it, which wasn't true.

At the end of the night we got the barber and carried him to the cab – he couldn't walk. He had a Polish woman with him who was a nutter and was screaming at him. He was too smashed to notice.

The next day I was in bed after it finished at 6am. It was like a horror film. There were glasses and bottles of drink everywhere. Cigarette ends, speakers, people lying all over the place. It looked like a war zone.

I carried on and it was up and down with her, even though we had that party. I was losing touch with her completely. A couple of weeks later I was in Colchester and I saw a car spares shop. It was as big as a supermarket. I thought, this is going to be the one. It was in a great spot. Not far from Colchester station. I met the landlord and he offered easy terms – a month's rent in and out. It was about £550 a week plus bills. It even had its own car park. It was a massive place with a loading bay. He had a car spares mail order business and was moving to smaller premises. He was a nice fella. I was going to do a furniture shop and auction there. I told her, she didn't want to know. There was bad friction. I gave him a deposit of £500, which I lost. She went all distant on me.

I had big plans for that place. It would have been a great move in my life but obviously the coke got in, along with the rowing. Little did I know she had other plans, that she didn't want to stay with me. Obviously, I never knew about it. I knew something was up, but not what.

About a week after that, we weren't getting on at all. It was up and down. I went home one night from the shop and there was a note from Harwich police. It said can you come down, we want to ask you a few questions about something. It's "nothing to worry about", they said. It was about three weeks after the fight, and was Martin's 17th birthday. I'd come from the shop and I had £5,000 in my pocket. I went around there and the copper said, "We had a complaint the other week from the council about noise pollution from the party." He said it's nothing to worry about, he said we just want to clear up a few things with you. I said, fine. He asked about the fight and I said I don't know about that, because I'm not stupid. He said, "Well, come through and have a chat, and you'll be out in five minutes." I went in the room, which I thought was odd because if it's nothing serious you talk at the counter. I was in there for two minutes and he said, "I'm arresting you for GBH and ABH. I've got four witnesses. You attacked Mr and Mrs so and so." I thought, fucking hell.

Straightaway I said no comment. He took me to Clacton police station to charge me.

He said, "Don't worry, I'll drop you back to your house afterwards." I thought that's all right, but in the back of my mind I remembered when we had a bit of drama about some moody cheques in Haverhill. A court case when I didn't turn up for a second appearance. It was to do with the modelling agency. It was nothing, but I didn't go back to court. When I was in Clacton police station I gave my full name. The bloke on the desk said, "I'm arresting you for GBH, ABH", etc. In the meantime, they took my money and my belt. He said, we'll be done in half an hour. He came back in and said, "Do us a favour, can you lift your shirt up?"

The second he saw my tattoo, he arrested me straightaway. I knew the second he asked me. He went, "You're in trouble." I said, "No comment." He said, "Cambridgeshire police have been looking for you for two years for a minor incident when you never returned to court." I said, I don't know anything about that. They kept me in there for two days. They brought Karen in as well and held her for two days. My mum had the kids. They said to me, you've got to take responsibility for the fight. My response was, "Bollocks, no comment." They eventually let Karen out after two days but they kept me inside.

Four days later the Old Bill came down from Bury St Edmunds. The double-handcuffed me, which I thought was a bit much. They then took me down to Bury St Edmunds police station, where I was held for another two days. I appeared in front of a judge at Cambridge crown court, who said, "You're wanted for a fraud charge", and refused me bail. They wanted me to make a statement but I refused. At the time, I had a duty solicitor, some 22-year-old who normally does parking tickets. I thought, "What the fuck does he know? I'm keeping my mouth shut."

After that they took me to Bedford nick, but it was full. They had me in the holding cell until 6pm before they put me on the bus with all the heroin addicts shouting and screaming as they're going cold turkey. It was full, so we went to Peterborough. We got there about 7.30pm. It's a privately run prison by Sodexo, so all the officers are freshly out of Sainsbury's, with shiny shoes. I thought "This is fucking great."

To start with I was on the induction wing. They put me with this really camp gay bloke who was in for growing weed. He was a bit of a nutter who had threatened someone with a shotgun, apparently. He said, "Oh, what are you in for?" I said, "Don't even talk to me." He went, "I'll make a brew." He wasn't a bad fella, but he told me his life story. It was a 23-hour lockdown prison. On the first night, he barricaded himself in the cell. He went into one over something they weren't giving him. He pressed the buzzer on the wall and they came down, but he barricaded himself in. They told me to stay in my bed. About eight prison guards came in, and I didn't see him again.

Next they moved in a wannabe gangster from Luton. He kept saying, "When we get out we'll have to meet up." I wasn't up for that. There were a lot of foreigners there. It even had rabies.

I was there three days, and they said they're shutting the wing down. A big black geezer three doors down from me got murdered. The punctured his lung and stamped on him over £10 of methadone, because they sell it in there. Three of them did it. I was off the gear and didn't feel too clever. I was coming round to reality and thinking about my son's birthday, my mum not being well, and the problems I was having with Karen.

After a week, they put me on the main wing. The second day I was there two mixed-race fellas in their mid 30s came up to me and asked, "Where are you from, bruv?" I said, "One, I'm not your brother and two, what the fuck has it got to do with you?" One of them shaped up and I went, "Mate, you better leave it." I thought we were going to fight, but they swallowed and then they didn't come anywhere near me at all.

My experience there was that they'd beat the fuck out of you for a Mars bar. It was a dreadful place, where they preyed on weak people. Luckily for me I stood my ground. When I was on the main wing they gave me the single cell where that gay bloke apparently got beaten to a pulp by some other inmates. You get a key for your cell there when you go out, so other inmates don't nick your stuff. I met a bloke called Paul Finch, he had a bit of trouble over Subutex. He was a very educated man and had spent a lot of time in Goa in India. He was a likable fella but a heroin addict. He got arrested in Ipswich after they caught him with two wraps of heroin.

One day he came into my cell and said he had a bit of trouble. Some fellas came in his cell and took his moody watch. He owed them about £15. When I was with him two of them came in the cell. A big northern fella started throwing his weight around. I told him in no uncertain terms to fuck off. Things got a little bit messy. I said "I'll throw you over the balcony" and they swallowed. Maybe I was lucky, maybe I wasn't. That Paul was victimised, so I felt sorry for him because he couldn't look after himself. He started crying. I said, when you come out of here get in contact with me and I'll sort you out with some work.

After four months, they took me back to court. This time I got bail on condition that I surrender my passport. It was a bit harsh for a fraud charge. The other charges were still pending, but when I was out I had to sign on at the police station in Clacton every day.

They knew me in there, it was 200 yards from my shop, the custody sergeant bought furniture off me. They said, "What are you doing in here?"

One day Karen came to court with my nephew. The judge gave me conditional bail, but they couldn't find my passport. They said you've got until the end of the day to find your passport, or you're going back to prison. They just managed to find it in time. I came out that night.

I bought a quarter of gear and two bottles of Dom Perignon Rose champagne for £700. It was the longest I've done for years off the gear. The police still had my £5,000. They refused to give me the cash back and eventually gave me a cheque. I took it to Cash Converters. They charged me £200 to cash it but I didn't care, I just wanted my money.

The police carried on making their inquiries. I was going through a very rough patch with her. She was fucking around with someone. She was getting more and more involved with that woman and Dyson. She'd say "I'm going to bingo" or something like that. What the fuck, she'd never been to bingo in her life. I was getting a little bit concerned. I thought, this is bollocks. I had two kids there, they were saying "What's happening, Dad?" The shop was sliding away because my mind was all over the place. She was fucking about. I was still using gear quite heavy. She went missing a few nights, and things got way out of control.

I got a phone call and Paul was released, and he was waxing furniture with Martin upstairs. Paul came round and did gear with me on a regular basis. He even said to me, you want to calm down with her.

I got a call from the police station and they charged me. They also charged Karen, Ken the barber, the DJ and the singer with assault. I was looking at three to five years in prison and I thought the game was up.

At the same time, me and Karen really felt apart. I confronted her and said "You're really fucking me about." I stood my ground. It was painful, but it needed to be done. One night I said to her, "Your stuff is loaded in the van." I'd just bought a new Datsun van, and I got the kids to do it to educate them. It was a very difficult to do. I said, "There's your gear, now fuck off." I had the two kids outside, crying. I said, "They're staying with me." They said, "We don't want to go with you, mum." She drove back to her mum's in Woodford and that woman's in Clacton.

I saw her out and about a bit. She was ringing me up saying, "I'm sorry, I want to come home." I fucked her off. It was painful, but that was a bad moment in my life. I spent five nights in a room on the gear after we split. I locked myself in there, never opened the shop. It was a fucking bad time.

She was begging to come back. I was still taking money, but it was difficult. I met a few women in there. I met a mad woman called Alison. She was only 32, but was number two on the list for doing gear. She had three kids. Karen knew her because she always used to come in for the gear. I rang her up one night. She said, come and pick me up. I did and we bought a quarter of gear, did that, so I bought another quarter. I ended up shagging the arse off her. That was a massive sex-fest, not that I remember much of it. I remember I woke up next to her, naked.

My son said, "I don't like her, she's got a mouth like a sewer." Another woman had just come over from Marbella. A blonde woman, she looked like Joanna Lumley but younger, about 40s. I sold her a sofa bed. She was on the gear. I took her out to the Pier restaurant. She was in good nick because she used to be a showgirl for DJ Johnny Walker. Karen was still ringing me to come back.

While all this was happening the court case came up. I never got a brief. I said, "Why do I want someone who doesn't know what day it is? I'm not making any statements, just my name and date of birth." That was it. When I went to court Karen was on the phone. She wouldn't talk to me because I wasn't with her. The barber and singer were there. No one would talk to me. I had my two kids in the public gallery waiting to see what was going to happen. The case went on for three days and eventually the judge threw it out. The police hadn't done something properly so it collapsed. The statements were incorrect so the judge threw it out. He said, "I'm dismissing this case, you are free to go." I couldn't believe it, I didn't even have to go in the dock.

The others weren't so lucky. Karen got a suspended sentence and the others got community service. The barber got arrested at 10am cutting someone's hair. He got thrown out of the Freemasons over it. I thought I was in trouble there, but somehow I managed to get out of it. I remember when I was walking out of the dock. There were four of us in there. The DJ was shitting himself, he'd never had a parking ticket in his life. I went to him "You're going to prison, mate." He started crying. I said, "That's what happens when you open your mouth."

I walked out of with my two boys. I had to go back to court for the dodgy cheques but I paid £8,000 gladly and walked away a free man.

Karen was still ringing me up on a regular basis.

Just after I'd won the case I started having trouble with my landlady. She never told me, but she wanted to build flats at the top of the garden. I only found out when I went up there one day and saw the planning application on the garage door. I said fuck it, I'm not having it no more.

I started looking for somewhere else when I spotted another house in Clacton. It was about £1,000 a month and owned by a woman called Belinda. It was completely new and had all white surfaces. It was kitted out. It was a four-bed. She was Turkish and lived in Epping. Someone came in my shop and told me about it. I was in there within two weeks. I got my two boys and the vans. And that's where I got really bad with the gear.

CHAPTER 22

—

MOVING ON
FROM KAREN

When Karen left I really went off the rails with the gear. Somehow I still ran the shop, but it was a hard time. Coming out of a long-term relationship was a big shock. Even though I'd ended it, I still spent a lot of time thinking about things. You wonder if she's with anyone else. Is it my fault we split up? How is it affecting the kids? It's all running through your mind at a million miles an hour. To cope, I turned to the gear even more. I'm not blaming anyone for the fact that I put my head down on a kitchen work surface and did £800 of coke. That was my choice. But the situation I was in, and my drug habit, meant I turned to it even more.

When I split up with Karen I spent five days up on the gear. That became a regular occurrence in those first few months after we split. I was still often high when I went to work. I was making a good living, but I was barely keeping it together. I was using coke heavily to try and numb the pain. It was my angle to escape. Some people numb the pain with a pint, others use coke. I had both.

The second house we moved in was pretty flash. It was in the nice bit of Clacton, not the end full of cider drinkers and teenage mums. We were looking to move out and a customer came into the shop and said, "I know someone who's got a lovely house in Clacton." The landlady was from Buckhurst Hill, which I knew well. It was an absolutely brand spanking new five-bed. It had solid oak floors throughout, and a massive kitchen with a big work station in the middle. Not that I ever did much cooking. It had en-suite showers, marble bathrooms, integrated work appliances, self-closing kitchen doors and marble work surfaces. It was the bollocks. The first time I went to see it they told me it was £1,000 a month, and I took it on the spot.

As soon as I got in there everything went haywire there because I started drinking very heavily during the week, after work. I was getting on the wine every night, and with that came the coke. I was having people round, and the party scene kicked off again. Paul Finch, the heroin addict who I met in prison, came round a lot. He was still on heavy drugs at this point. I never saw him do it in my house and if I had I would have thrown him through the fucking window, but I'm sure he was still taking heroin. When he came round we did a lot of coke together. He loved the stuff, so he was coming round regularly. He was great company, but his habits just made me take more gear. By this point I was spending about £1,000 a week on the stuff. After I'd paid my bills there wasn't a lot left. It was ridiculous, and getting out of control. As I took more and more gear the business started slipping. Things weren't getting done, or were getting done late. The shop was running low on stock and I wasn't going up to London to buy any more. I was opening late, or not bothering to go in some days, depending how bad my hangover was. I couldn't be bothered. It didn't matter to me any more.

To compensate for splitting up with Karen I started hooking up with a few distasteful women. Most of them I met through the shop. I've already mentioned one nutty bird in particular called Alison, who was a raving lunatic. She was a pretty girl who had a good heart, but she had loads of issues. She had three kids and was constantly having trouble with them. She told me her life story while we were together, about how her parents split up when she was young and sent her to a home. She loved the gear, and despite only being 32 one of the biggest coke-heads I ever met. She was in my top three and only slightly behind Dyson. She could do gear all night, no issue.

Sometimes we'd stay up for days sniffing coke and drinking, talking bollocks, as you do.

She was seeing a psychiatrist because she had mental health problems. I didn't know at the time. It was only later on that I learned she wasn't right, but when you're on a rebound you'll take what you can get. As well as coke she liked to drink, beer especially. I woke up one morning and she was drinking a can of Stella at 8am. Work that one out for yourself. She was a bit of an oddball, but I'm not going to run her down because I had fun with her.

Eventually that fizzled out because she got to be a nuisance, ringing up the shop pissed, and I thought fuck that.

After that finished another woman came in the shop and bought a sofa bed off me. She was a bit older, in her 50s. She used to be a dancer, and still had a great body.

We'd only been in that house for about eight months when things really started to unravel. I would often go to work so high I could barely function. If you have 30 lines of coke you're still going to be off your tits the next day. There's no way you can be normal. Even though you say you can function, in reality you're all over the place. Your decisions are terrible, your judgement is awful. The thoughts in your mind take you to be somewhere else. Obviously, you've got serious problems in your mind. The break-up, and looking after two kids, all gets too much. It's all a lot to take on board.

I got through it by using coke as a substitute to guide me through. That was my avenue to escape, which is a very sad thing to say. At that house I was drinking beer, which was unusual for me. I've always liked to drink, but I've always been a bit of a connoisseur. I used to drink champagne and fine wine, not cheap shit. When I was there I started drinking cans of beer, which I'd never done before. It was because Alison used to drink beer. Even though I was an alcoholic I'd always have a nice bottle of wine or ten. I wouldn't get four cans and hang around outside Morrisons with the other scumbags. But that changed when I was there, and things just got worse and worse.

I began to stop caring.

As things really began to fall apart, I had a stroke of luck. A couple of fat fellas called Rob and Gary, who ran a market store in Clacton, came into the shop one day and asked me where I got the furniture from. I told them to fuck off and said, "What are you doing coming in here, trying to get my stuff off me?" Rob came back and apologised, and we started chatting. I said, "We might be coming out of here." They agreed to take my business off me, and I gave them all my contacts for £15,000. They made it work, and I think they're still there now. I introduced them to the landlord, who was a fucking nutter. Her son came in one day and got all funny with me. I straightened things out eventually and we walked away with money.

CHAPTER 23

—

ROCHFORD

I wanted to move back to London after Clacton, because that's where I'm from and I wanted to go back to my roots. But by this stage my parents were living on Canvey Island. My mother had just been diagnosed with breast cancer and really wasn't well, so I decided to stay in Essex. During my house search I bumped into a very attractive blonde estate agent called Lisa. We clicked straightaway and she later invited me to a party, where it all kicked off. She found me a lovely five-bed house in Rochford, which I duly accepted. It needed decorating but it was a nice four-storey townhouse with a loft conversion and a big garden in a cul de sac.

By the time we moved from there my mother was very ill. She had an operation for her cancer and it seemed like things were getting better. But within weeks she'd had an aneurism, which meant she could die at any moment. She looked dreadful. She was still upset about the break-up, being an old- school mother. She was very staunch, rare as rocking-horse shit, and even though she didn't like Karen she thought we should have stuck it out. At the same time my dog Bomber was getting ill too. It couldn't have come at a worse time, and was really affecting me. That just meant I kept heavy on the powder and drink. As always I was hoping to make a fresh start, but old habits quickly crept in. I was heavy on the coke, and without a shop open every day my lifestyle got more and more out of control.

After we moved into Rochford I kept on selling cars and doing the odd bit of furniture. I rented a big double garage out near Benfleet where I used to flog it from. I was advertising in sweetshops for 50p a go. Putting those ads in shop windows is very effective because people looked in them, and they still do. I was also buying lineage in local newspapers. I was selling double beds for £180 and buying them for £90, so I was doubling my money. I was selling unused double beds, still in the wrapper, for £165. They used to retail at £399, so I sold quite a few. I was still selling a few Mercs out of the house too, which meant I was ticking over. Most weeks I'd turn £2,000, all cash.

The drinking there was very heavy, and the cocaine went up another gear. I was spending all my money on coke. I was having drinking sessions four nights a week. I was taking coke Wednesday to Sunday, then recovering Monday and Tuesday before I got back on it. I was still mingling with different women on a regular basis. I went through quite a few mostly mental women. I was having a lot of one-night stands. It was getting a bit messy round there. I was doing at least £800 a week coke by myself. It was about £1,000 an ounce in those days. I was staying up for days and days at a time. I used to have very heavy sessions. I could start at 6pm on a Friday and still be going strong on Sunday afternoon. Once or twice I did an ounce of gear in 24 hours. That's 28g, which is a lot of gear. You should be dead, but because the gear has been cut it wasn't that strong. Luckily enough for me. Had it been even 60 per cent pure I'd be dead.

Your body can't take that kind of punishment. You're going to have a heart attack, it's going to explode. When I was doing coke there I was using vodka and wine very heavily. Every weekend I had these mad benders on Friday and Saturdays. I'd wake up on Sunday afternoon and feel like shit, with some woman I barely knew lying next to me. I had a lot of undesirable blokes in the house. Most of them were plastic gangsters. No one ever gave me any trouble. I had always been able to make people understand that I'm not a man to be taken for a fool. But that didn't stop it getting out of control.

The boys were floating about with me, not going to school. Martin didn't need to go to school at this point, but Albert should have still been in school. The truant officers caught up with me while I was there, and started demanding to know when he was going to school. They were threatening me with prosecution unless he went to school. One day one of them said, "The only way you can get out of it is by having a private tutor." I did that for a while. They came round a couple of times and it fizzled out. The council gave up in the end – he wasn't far off 16, and they didn't really give a fuck. The boys ended up being with me full-time selling the cars, cleaning them, and selling a bit of furniture. All the while my mum was getting more and more ill. When she got really poorly they moved her to Southend Hospital, where I went to see her for what would be the last time. I was in there for five seconds and I walked out. I left my car in the car park. I couldn't cope with it.

To see a woman that you've idolised who brought you up as a child reduced to five stone and not even recognise you isn't nice. I never went into the hospital drunk, but I'd had a heavy night and I couldn't cope seeing her like that. When I went in there I had to summon all my energy and bravery and courage to see her. I've never been a man who's gone to hospitals. Seeing her in there was one of the worse moments of my life. It's probably the worst. I walked out in bits. I broke down crying. It was a terrible experience.

That's the last time I saw my mother, God rest her soul.

After that she went to a hospice in Southend for terminally ill people. I never went there in the three months before she died. People used to say, "How can't you go and see your mum?" But that was my choice. It was my choice to remember a woman as a flourishing beautiful, kind woman, smiling with her son. Why would I want to remember her as a four-stone bag of bones who doesn't recognise me? She didn't have Alzheimer's, but the cancer spread throughout her body and sent her mad. It sounds rude and disrespectful not to see your mother on her death bed, but I couldn't do it.

I thought I wouldn't have any more trouble with the Old Bill after Harwich, but I was wrong. In Clacton we had a furniture bank account. Apparently, I'd written some dodgy cheques out which I didn't even know about. The Old Bill came round to the Rochford house and arrested me on Martin's 17th birthday. They didn't take it any further and I got released the day after, but it just seemed like cruel fate. After the last time, I thought "You are fucking joking." It was about 6am. I was off my nut after a heavy night on the powder. They took me to Southend police station and held me there. I didn't make any comment and they released me the next day.

Not long after that I got invited to a party by the attractive estate agent who found me the house. Her husband had a massive place in Thorpe Bay, Southend. She invited me and told me to bring some gear. She had a massive house with a swimming pool with all Versace furniture. Her husband was a right prick. He knew she fancied me. That was a terrible evening. We were up until 7am, everyone in the party was doing gear. I ended up going back to my house in Rochford with a bloke and a woman who were a right pair of nutters. I nearly had a little bit of trouble with them after they started getting funny. It was about 7.30am and they started making a few sarky comments, so I fucked them off and they shit themselves. I remember having a row with them outside. Her husband was on about buying some coke.

I'd been feeding them all night, so I told them to fuck off if they knew what was good for them. They did. After that I got a message from the landlady saying she wanted to sell it. I think there might have been a little bit of spiteful injection from the woman who had the party. I think the landlady was lying and just wanted me out.

CHAPTER 24

—

SOUTHEND

W e moved out of there and then we moved into another road in Halifax Drive, Southend. I spotted it after the landlady gave me a month's notice. I met the landlord, who was a very wealthy man. He was a right fucking lunatic who drove a 1930s car. He was tight beyond belief, but he was pretty staunch. He met me, shook my hand, I said it was me and my two boys. I don't like being fucked about and all that bollocks. I told him about the dog, which he didn't have a problem with.

We moved in there, and unfortunately that particular house where almost where my mum passed away. When the person is taken away to heaven before the funeral you can go and see them. I didn't do it. When she was cremated I walked out halfway through the ceremony. There were loads of people in there with crocodile tears, no good mugs. All crying their eyes out, pretending to be upset. I just thought "You bunch of pricks." My dad was there. I've only seen him cry a couple of times in my entire life. He broke down, which wasn't a nice experience. It was one of the most cruel and sad experiences that I had ever encountered in my lifetime. She stuck with him for 55 years through thick and thin. They loved each other in their own way.

Within weeks of my mum dying, Bomber died. He was eight, but his back legs went. I remember I was up all night, and he was crying out in pain because he couldn't get up. I was in bits. I looked out of the window and he managed to get up and look at me. That killed me. I walked out of the house. I fucked off. I had to get my dad round there. He got the vet out and they put him to sleep and let him run free.

The trauma caused me to go off the Richter scale. I went turbo. I was up for five nights completely coked out of my head. I didn't speak to anyone. Everyone stayed clear of me because they know

I can be a little bit mental. I kept looking at pictures of my mother with tears rolling down my face, regretting not going to see her, but obviously that was my choice. I don't regret it to this day, because I wouldn't want to remember my mum as a four-stone bag of bones who couldn't talk. It's not a nice way to remember your parents as far as I'm concerned. Other people say different. They say they brought you into the world, you should sit by them until the end.

That's their choice.

My choice is the way I've dealt with it. Obviously, later on in life I've suffered with that. I wouldn't say I've got regrets, but I've thought about doing things differently. She was my mother, and she stood by me through thick and thin. When my mum passed we had a service in Pitsea and they took her to be with her family in Manor Park, because they're from East London. After the service, we went into the pub. My dad was in there, in bits. It was a fucking horrible thing. After that I went overboard, as I say I went turbo on the coke and booze, trying to soften the blow of losing my mother. I was hitting the coke really hard, trying to block it out of my mind.

My dad wasn't coping very well either, which isn't surprising after the woman he'd lived with for 55 years died. I was trying to do what I could, but I didn't have great contact with my family at this point. I've always been a private man and done my own business. They've always wanted to know me when I had a few quid. But when the shit hits the fan people tend to disappear and leave you to fight your own battles yourself. I was in no position to do that because I was under the influence of coke and drink. I was in a bad place but I was still trying to do my best to cover my end. There were a lot of sad memories in that house and I was very drunk.

My mind was in overdrive when my mum died. I kept thinking about that, the break-up with Karen and my kids. It meant my businesses took a back step. I was still making money because I've always been a man to turn a pound note, but money was going out as fast as it was coming in. I was spending up to £1,000 a week on coke. It wasn't like one gram on a Friday night, I'd stay up and do £400 by myself no problem. I could do one gram in one line with one nostril. I'm not proud of it and it's a horrendous an horrific thing to admit, but it's true. Most people would get 15 lines out of one gram if you cut it really thin with a Stanley blade. I'd crush it with a credit card and do one fat line with one gram. That goes straight into your system, whether it's strong or cut to fuck. You get an explosive reaction, and within ten minutes it hits you. Think about it, you're doing ten lines in one hit. Most people do one line and they're off their tits. Their jaw is all over the place. I've done two grams in two lines on a regular basis.

In that house my daily routine would be getting up at about 10.30am and checking the phone for messages. I'd get a junk breakfast at the local café, which was why I was overweight. I was a smart man with a bit of style, even though I lost my pride and confidence on the gear so I did try and wear nice clothes and keep myself in order. I still put a massive amount of weight on there. I went up to 18 stone. I was eating junk food, cooked breakfast every day. I was a 42 waist, I'm now 32 inches. I'd wake up, go down the café, have shit junk food. I was smoking about 30 cigarettes a day, which was rare for me. I was still selling the odd car here and there, and a bit of furniture. I was keeping my head above water, I don't know how, but I was.

Monday I'd still be recovering from Friday and Saturday. Then when you go into Tuesday and Wednesday and I'd have a bottle of Smirnoff. I remember a few occasions when I'd drink two large bottles of Smirnoff by myself in one night. I would wake up absolutely stinking of vodka. I consumed more alcohol just to push out my nightmares of my mother. The more I was drinking, the more coke I took. You can't drink and not take coke. Some people do, but I used to do both. I was a binge drinker and I used to cane the fuck out of it. I'd see people have six vodkas and I'd think, fuck, I'll do three bottles of wine, seven grams of coke, half a bottle of champagne, and I'd still be up at 7am watching a dirty video. That's the way things used to roll.

It slowly got worse and I gathered more weight through my terrible lifestyle, awful diet, dabbling with rough women and mingling with undesirable characters. None of them were gangsters, they were two-bob mugs, but when you're in that situation you tend to attract different characters. Some are all right, but most are bullshitters. Some are two-bob gangsters that work in Asda and think they're Al Capone. I went through that stage, and it got very sad because I could see myself deteriorating to a point where I was getting concerned. My face was red. I was bloated. I didn't have a lot of inspiration to do a lot, just sell the odd car here and there.

The boys were still on board, I respect them for that. My dad was going through a rough time. I wasn't getting a great deal of support from my own family. It was a difficult time, and probably the point where I took the most cocaine. I did a couple of stints in that house when I couldn't get any more gear up my nose and I was eating it off a teaspoon.

One particular night I was sitting there by myself with the TV on and I thought "Fucking hell, I've already seen this programme." I'd gone right round the clock. I was watching the news again.

I never even knew. I was sitting there sniffing coke, drinking. I couldn't believe what was going on. I stayed up for the rest of the day. I went across the road to get another two bottles of wine and went back indoors and I was in a bad way. I was drinking it out of the bottle like a hobo. I was an old has-been, looking through a lot of photographs of my previous life. I was having a lot of flashbacks about my mother, thinking about relationships that didn't work, the list goes on.

That house was a terrible place for me because my dog died there too. He meant a lot to me because I love dogs and always have done. I might come across as this big tough character but if you get to know me, which isn't easy, I'm not. It was mental torture there. I couldn't get out of the rut of taking cocaine, or pull myself out of a situation where I'm fucked. You've got nowhere to turn apart from get another wrap of coke or another drink because, you're in that terrible click of being a coke addict and an alcoholic. It's a very dark place to be, especially when you've fallen a long way.

I had a lot of wealth in my previous life, and it was going very quickly. The drug intake was going through the roof. My health was deteriorating. My thoughts, my confidence, my sharpness and my keen-as-mustard persona was deteriorating very quickly. Sometimes I saw it myself in the cold light of day, and realised what a sad place I was in. No fucker wants to help you. They just want to sit there doing your coke, drinking, and talking like gangsters. Talking shit about who they know, who they don't, and putting the world to rights. It's very difficult to get out of that cycle if you're with people like that. You can move, but everywhere you go you can obtain cocaine and alcohol. If you've got a bit of banter about you, it's the simplest thing in the world.

My mind was destroyed in that house. I was there about four months when my mum died. My boys saw me in a bad way. They saw me breaking down because I was fed-up and drinking. I've always had a very strong mindset, but they saw that crumble. It was a terrible place to be. They were a bit older, and I couldn't pull the wool over their eyes. They see things, and they think when they're a bit older and look into things. I was always drunk, with some old bird lying about. It wasn't the nicest place for a young teenager.

I couldn't deal with the impact of my mother dying. I can take most things on the chin, not many things shock or scare me. It never has and never will. But that did. I coped with it through taking more cocaine and drinking more alcohol to hide my sadness, and the reality check that my mother's gone, my life has gone down the pan and I'm still using drugs. I am now a weak person because the drugs have taken full control. I am the passenger, they are the driver. When I was there, I couldn't wait to get home to order a bit of gear.

On a Thursday and Friday I'd get home and think "Fuck, I've got to make that phone call." I'd be waiting on the corner for my gear off the geezer. I'd get in and bang, have a couple of lines and feel so much better. If you asked me today about it and put a line of coke in front of me, knowing what I've gone through, I'd break your jaw. I'm not a bully-boy, but I'd have no hesitation because I've been through so much shit with the gear. I've seen the misery, the sadness, the nightmares that still exist in my mind to this day through taking gear. After everything I've been through it would be a disgraceful thing to do. I wouldn't want to be in the same room as anyone who had coke. The stuff makes me feel physically sick now. I get flashbacks. My heart starts beating. They are very sad and distressing flashbacks. Most people who been through what I have would have a breakdown. I had a meltdown, sniffing coke and drinking. It was too much to take on board.

Monday was for recovering so I'd eat shit food, probably a pizza or KFC. The boys would get some grub in. Martin would cook a bit. I'd probably get a takeaway in. Smoking like a trooper. I wouldn't touch any gear on Monday, but sometimes I did: if I had a little bit left over I'd have a couple of cheeky lines. The thing with cocaine is, you have two lines and you're under starter's orders. You can't just have a bit. Two lines, and I'm going to the off-licence to get a bottle of vodka, I'm calling my dealer, some skank round the corner. Then you're up and running. Often Mondays would be about recouping. I'd stink, sitting on the sofa, bars of chocolate on the floor, bottles of pop on the floor.

Tuesday I would try and get myself together, but with cocaine it's never the day after. It's the day after that when it hits you. If you took it tonight, tomorrow you wouldn't feel that bad. Wednesday you'd say "I feel terrible. My kidneys are hurting. I'm having negative thoughts, my stomach is all over the place, my eating is all over the gaff." That's what happens, it' s 48 hours later when it kicks in. The day after, you don't feel too bad because you're still semi-buzzing. You aren't off your tits, but you are semi-buzzing. But when you crash, you're fucked. On Tuesday I'd think about how I'd make some money. My phone would be off, so I'd check it. I'd try and get things sorted to make some money.

Come Wednesday, that's it. I'm up and running. Bottle of vodka, get one gram in, if I made a bit of money selling a car or a bit of furniture. So Wednesday the party would get started. We'd finish about 2am, so not too late. It wouldn't be an Eddie Murphy, because he did a film called *48 Hours*. By 2am, I'd probably be on my own or with one of my pals.

Thursday I'd wake up about midday feeling rough as fuck. I'd say, "I ain't touching the gear tonight." Come about 7pm I'd think "Fuck that, the weekend's here." I'd buy two bottles of vodka, a bottle of wine, because my money wasn't as accessible as before when I was buying £150 bottles of wine. I was buying three for £10. Cheap and cheerful, which isn't a great move. I buy a couple of grams, it would probably be a 4am job on Friday.

I'd wake up the next day and feel rough as fuck. "I ain't doing it for the weekend", I'd say. Come Friday evening I'd get a phone call off one of my pals, asking me if I wanted to go out for a drink. I'd go and meet them in a wine bar or pub. It wasn't really my sort of thing, so I'd invite them back for a couple of lines. Then it would be 7am in the morning.

I'd be in bed all day Saturday, laying up until 9am. I might have a couple of lines on a Saturday if I had anything left, and then I'd start again on the Sunday.

It was like the Lottery, it just rolled over from one day to the next. One week to the next. Some weeks I'd get on it on Monday night. That then rolls into Tuesday. You have a rest Wednesday and then back on it Thursday, Friday and Saturday. It was about six days on, one day off. It was a never-ending story. There was never going to be a moment when it was out of your system. You're going to be intoxicated with alcohol, or very depressed because the cocaine is slowly running you low on fuel. That's how it works. You just carry on and on. In the end, to be totally honest – and not many people say this – many people who get off cocaine say it gets so fucking boring. It's the same thing over and over again. You feel rough, low and depressed. Your pride is gone. Your head has gone. Your decisions are shit. Your judgement is terrible. You look around you, and the company you're keeping is terrible. You're knocking yourself. You keep blaming yourself for things you can't get away from, and blaming others for your mistakes.

You say you'll never do it again, but then you do it again because the drug kidnaps you. If you're a heavy user, like I was, it kidnaps you and you can't get away from it. People talk about twelve-step plans and rehab. It didn't work for me – I couldn't connect with the people on it. No disrespect to them, but I'm not sitting there with 15 other addicts. How is that going to help me? It's going to bring me down. I heard people come into rehab and buy two grams of coke off someone who's in there. That's not for me. I was spending a lot of money on coke. I was also feeding other people's habits.

I've always been a very generous man, and I was paying for them. I always used to buy the whole bar a drink. Maybe it was a bit of a wide-boy, flamboyant thing to do, but everyone's got their own personality. It's not a bad thing to be a generous man. Being a tight cunt, to me you're no good. I used to have a few leeches around me. I knew it at the time, but I didn't make it known to them, not wanting to put the frighteners on them. When you're on the gear you say "Don't worry about it, mate, crack on. Put your money away, I'll have a bit of that." That's how it went, on and on.

Slowly but surely, they disappear when the money and the gear run out. They move on to the next victim them. I even thought about that back then. Being taken for a mug, coming from the background that I've come from, hit me really hard. I couldn't take it on board, but I just kept going. Kept using the gear, drinking, same boring shit. Same boring stories, same bollocks talk, the same shit people. It's a never-ending story.

I fell out with a few people there, and cleared off. I was there for 18 months. I was on a night out, and a bit of an argument broke out over nothing. I was in a wine bar with a friend of mine called Brian, who died. He was an alcoholic. Someone had a little dig at my mate, who was overweight. I was overweight too, so we had a bit of a fall-out. It got a bit out of hand, but not for me, for them. It carried on, and we had a bit of a get-together outside. I came away without losing, but then I heard that these people are coming back and they're going to single me out. Nothing ever materialised, but that's what you get in Essex.

I fell out with a couple of women too. One was called Penny. She was a headcase, and another Hoover. She was in my top five. She sniffed more gear than anyone I knew. She was 35, and I met her through one of my mates. I fucked her off, and she started making phone calls and banging on my door. It was a very short-lived thing, but I thought: "I've got to move away from here. I've got memories of my mother, my dog died here, I've got some nutty bird banging on the door." I'd had a row in the town with a couple of people, which wasn't an issue.

"But," I thought, "I've got to move on."

CHAPTER 25

—

COGGLESHAW

Iknew I needed to get out of Southend, so I started looking around for somewhere new. I saw an advert in a shop window in Witham after I went there to see a Mercedes. It was for a nice-looking cottage in Coggleshaw. The landlady was called Edith, from a family of builders. They owned half the street and were very strange people. She was no different, and must have inhaled too much lead paint as a child. That said, it was a very nice cottage, old though. It had crooked wooden floors and ceilings. It was all over the gaff, truth be told, but for £900 a month I took it. She said she was going to need a couple of references, which wasn't an issue, so I gave her a deposit and moved in.

Originally I was taking my two boys with me, but before we moved in Martin said to me he fancied living with his mate Ray in Colchester. He was about 17, and I was fine with him finding his feet. My son Albert moved in with me, but he didn't actually like it. The village is like *Emmerdale Farm*, and full of weirdoes. Unless your family have lived there for six generations you're an outsider. It's that type of place. After a few weeks he moved back in with his mother. She opened a baker's shop in Ilford after her mother stuck about £80,000 up. It had been there for years when she took it over and tried to transfer it into a café. She offered him a job there.

Martin never spoke to his mum from day one when we threw her out of Clacton. He hates the sight of her, and it's as simple as that. Albert was on and off with his mum. Martin is more like me, Albert is like his mum. When she offered him the job I said, "Go and do a few days there." He found one of her friends had a room to rent in a quiet house. I was happy with him setting himself up, even if it was with her. The business didn't last, but it was a good opportunity for him.

After I moved in alone I kept on selling a few cars and doing a bit of furniture. I was still using coke and drinking a lot. It got very bad down there because it was out the way. There was a pub across the road from my house, and the village had a very well-known restaurant which I went in frequently. I started going in there on my own, drinking champagne and getting on the gear. I met a few women in there. Had a few little turn-outs with a couple, to tell you the truth.

After about three or four weeks I went for a trim in the local hairdresser's. In there I spotted a pretty little blonde bird called Ruth. She caught my eye, so I turned on the old charm and within a couple of weeks I asked her out. She said yes, so I took her to a posh restaurant where we got on the drink. Afterwards she went back to mine and the rest is history. I was selling a few cars and furniture, and still getting on the gear. I kept on drinking heavily because there was a Coop next door. I'd always go round there and buy three bottles of wine for £10. Once I'd had half a bottle I'd want to get on the gear, and it would go from there. It wasn't as bad as before, but I'd be coked out of it from Thursday to Sunday without fail. I was still struggling to accept my mother's death, so I was drowning my sorrows on a regular basis. It wasn't a good place to be. I struck up a relationship with her, and that was going all right to start with, until she showed her true colours. She had a young kid by someone else.

I quickly realised she wasn't a normal woman. She was a bit mental, to say the least. She'd been on her own for six years, after the kid's father left her when he was one. She was in her 30s, but she'd spent most of her 20s as a stripper in London. She was a dancer at Spearmint Rhino, Stringfellow's, the lot, so she had all the right bits in the right places so to speak. She was a typical hairdresser who thought she knew everything. In reality the opposite was true.

I went out for a lot of meals with her and her kid. It was very difficult to connect with him, because he wasn't my child. Broken homes are never easy. We didn't get a lot of nights out because she needed a babysitter. For some reason, and I'll never know why, we got engaged. It wasn't like we were madly in love, so I still wonder to this day why we did it. I don't know what came over me to ask her. I didn't propose, but I said, "Do you want to get married?" After she said yes, I got her two wedding rings that cost £10,000 off an orthodox Jew I know who runs pawnbrokers. He's a very shrewd operator and runs Max Croft's Securities in Newbury Park. I'd sold him a gold Rolex a while before. It had a diamond dial, and I think I got £7,000 for it. At the time, I said I'd come back for it, but money was up and down so I never went back. When I went to buy the rings, he remembered me.

The wedding was in Glastonbury. She had about a hundred people, I had none. The vicar, who was called Bob, said, "I've never done a wedding in my life where no one's turned up." I said, "Well, I haven't told anyone." He laughed, but it was true. I was very secretive. I met her family at the wedding. Her dad, John, said to me, "What plans have you got for the future?" I went, "Plans? I don't know what you're talking about." Bearing in mind what she'd told me about her parents, I wasn't having any of it. They didn't like me. I said, "I don't plan my life, John." He said, "You've got to plan, and put things in place."

They were very dominating people, who liked everything to be laid out in order, like coffee at 11am, diner at 1pm, be in bed by 9pm. I thought, "Fuck off, I don't live like that." He tried to say that to me a few times that day: "What plans have you got for my daughter?" I said, "I don't make plans, I'm lucky to be alive. I take each day as I find it." He knew I'd been very wealthy before, because Ruth told him. He wanted me to start again.

I don't like people telling me what to do. Not from a man who's put his seven-year-old daughter out to foster because he thinks she's evil. I'm not going to listen to the likes of him, the fucking chancer. I'd rather listen to a lollipop man in the street. I put him right, and he didn't say any more.

The wedding didn't have any dramas. A couple of her family tried to get a bit lippy. One of them got a bit funny and aggressive, so I took him outside and squared him up. I didn't have a best man, and her son gave her the ring. I lost a bit of weight there. I went through a weird stage. I wasn't overweight there. My weight went up and down. A lot of people's weight is up and down on gear, because it's a strange thing. Your body is all over the place. One minute you're bloated, the next minute you're skinny, then fat. Then you're drinking. The more gear you take, they reckon you're supposed to lose weight, but it depends what sort of body you've got.

She was a fucking horrible woman, always putting pressure on me to get a big house. She would say, "I don't cook any dinners for my husband. You've got to cook your own food. I'm not your skivvy. I'm a grafter. I go to work every day. No one's putting money in my pocket. I bring my money to the table." She was a bit like that. She knew I'd been very wealthy, and she was on tenterhooks, taking a bit of a hit. I was getting money, but I wasn't living like I had been with Karen. I was ducking and diving, still keeping my head above water. She was a money-grabber who wanted a one-way ticket to paradise. She said to me, "Once you take me on board, you take my son too. Lock, stock and barrel." I should have walked away that night. We were getting pissed at a barbecue at her house. I never took it on board.

She was more of a drinker, drank a lot of wine, even before I met her. She said, "I do a bottle of wine a night, just to calm my nerves."

I didn't like her, she wasn't a nice woman. She had a nasty streak in her. She wouldn't make me a cup of tea. I don't know what made me go with her. I think because my mum went to heaven, my mind was all over the place. She was attractive, but I'd had better. She had big tits, but was a bit stumpy and had zero personality. A 10/10 twat. She was a know-it-all – all the women that work in Spearmint Rhinos know it all. Most of them are brasses. They've got an answer for everything, but they know fuck-all. Basically, when I was living round there she was getting a bit arsy, saying, "You'd better get some more money coming in here." In the end, she got really personal about my family and I said, "You want to call it a day, mate. You're out of your fucking depth."

The next morning, she said, "Things are getting out of control here." Smoking like a trooper, I said, "Here are the keys to your house, why don't you stick them up your arse?" I still had the cottage, so I moved back in there for a while. I was having words with her, because I was only across the road in the shop. We were still talking, but things weren't right. Eventually I said, "Let's call it a day." That's when I got really heavy on the gear and things really spiralled out of control. Not because of her. There was no lost love there, no spilt milk. It was a bad mistake, definitely on my part.

She wouldn't be for me, even if she was the last woman on the planet. How can you live with a woman who won't even make you a meal or do your washing? She won't even make you a cup of tea. She'll turn around and say, "I'm not cooking you any meals,

I'm not a mug." I'd never heard of it. Life is a bit of give-and-take. I'm not expecting someone to wipe my arse, but she wouldn't do anything. She'd say, "I'm an independent businesswoman." She had a little poxy hairdresser's that her dad lent her £6,000 to set up. She thought she was the queen of the castle. Don't make me laugh. It didn't last long. She got a bit personal with my dad, which I got the hump over. I rang her back because I wanted to get the rings to pay the hospice that cared for him. She said she'd already sold them. I wanted to give the money to them.

Money means nothing to me, and it never has.

My final words were, "You're a horrible cunt." That was the last time I spoke to her. She was ringing up my dad time and time again about the divorce. I nearly went for half her business, but then I thought, stick it up your arse. All you've got is three hairdryers and a poxy little hairdresser's. It's not exactly Nicky Park in Grosvenor Square. It's in Coggleshaw. All you can do is a grey rinse, and you think you're the dog's bollocks.

I was only there about 15 days. I got my clothes and gear. I told her to fuck off, she told me the same. I put a call into her about something. She said, "I've got people in place waiting to sort you out." I said, "Listen to me very carefully. I'll tell you once. Don't ever contact my father again, because you're out of your depth." I think she shit herself, and that was the end of that. The divorce went through pretty quickly. They sent the paperwork to my sister's house. I'd already been through it before with Karen. I was in a bad way at that time. I was getting out and about more. I was mingling with one of my mates from south London, and taking a hell of a lot of gear.

I wasn't living with her before the wedding. I had no intentions of giving my place up. But she said, "When we get married, you might as well move in." I thought, surely when you get married you live together. But she kept saying to me, "Why don't you live in your place, and come over at weekends?" I said, "What are you talking about? We're married. Are we going to sleep in separate beds?"

After 15 days we had a drama in the morning. She asked me if I had a minute. She said, "My son Mitchell's just been into the kitchen. She said there were two bits of bread in the bread bin last night. Now he wants to have two bits of toast with jam and peanut butter. Did you take the other piece?" I thought she was joking. I said to her, "I tell you what. I'm fucking guilty. Take me to the Old Bailey. Here's £5, go round to Tesco and buy yourself ten loaves of blue-and-white-striped bread, you tight cunt."

That got the ball rolling straightaway. We had very bad vibes from there on in. She was mad about sharing wine, lights being left on, anything could set her off. When we'd go out she'd say, "Don't lose the keys to my house." What made me laugh was, she lived in a little shithole in Braintree. Many times, if I was out she'd say, "Make sure you get yourself some dinner. There's no dinner here, I don't do any cooking. Do your own washing, too."

When I moved in with her I had an idea she was a bit of a nutter, but I didn't know she'd be like that.

When I moved in, it went completely off the Richter scale. The atmosphere was terrible. The son was giving me dirty looks, a seven-year-old boy. She was mollycoddling him, he wasn't even allowed out in the garden. She said, "Don't go out there, it's dangerous." Look at her history, and that tells you everything. Her mum and dad are Jehovah's Witnesses. She went to three different families when she was young. She didn't speak to her sister. She'd threatened her in letters. She used to slag off my family. My family is rough and ready, but we're proper East London people. It is what it is. We're generous people who help each other. Good-natured and principled. It isn't about taking things back. It was very difficult to deal with her. It was a bad split.

She's still there now, as far as I know. She was very conservative with her son. No one in the hairdresser's knew she was a dancer. It was one of those little villages, and if you get a parking ticket you're Ronnie Kray. When I lived there, they all thought I was a crook because of my accent. I shut my door and pay my bills, who gives a fuck. She's a very strange individual. She had a nasty streak in her. Not pleasant at all. It came to a very quick, abrupt ending. I was out of there and gone.

I went back to the cottage, stayed there for a bit. My mum's death was still on my mind. A massive part of my life had gone. I didn't have the opportunity to say goodbye to Ruth, because I was so wrapped up in drink and drugs. I'm very regretful, even to this day. I still think about it every day.

After we split, she rang up my dad and got a bit personal. When you're on gear and drink, bad judgement creeps in on everything from buying a car to getting married. You look back later and think, "What the fuck was I doing?" You think you're doing well, but you're not. You're functioning, but you're firing on two cylinders instead of six. It's the same thing. When you're using the powder you can function, but it's very difficult. You cut corners, get things done quicker. You can't be bothered and you say, "Fuck that, I'll do it tomorrow." So you make mistakes.

It's taken its toll on me, and I've paid a high price for it. I'm still paying for it, and not just financially but mentally. Not physically. The strain and upset of it all affects you for the rest of your life. You can pull out of it. But I still think about things. I don't sit there and cry, but I think things could have been different. At the end of the day, you get dealt a hand of cards and you've got to play them the best you can. Mine were dealt to me, I turned away and dealt my own, and made my own mistakes that put me in that position.

I'm not going to blame myself. The marriage was a severe, savage experience. A lot of people say they've never known anyone married for such a short period. We did a quick divorce thing on the internet for £350. She sent me the papers. I wasn't going to sign them at first. I thought I'd take her to court for half her business. But then I thought, fuck it, I don't want to see your face again. She said she'd pay for it. I didn't want her to do me any favours, so I paid my share. I'd already experienced it with Karen. I didn't speak to her again, apart from the rings when I put her in her place.

I've had no contact since. I've had no reason to. If I won the lottery for £100 million I wouldn't give her 5p. I'd rather give it to a tramp. That's one of the worse experiences I've had with a woman, and I've had many bad experiences with women. I was spending £500 a week on coke and £200 a week on wine. I spent a lot of money in the restaurant there, too. The bloke who owns it is on *Masterchef*. I used to sit in the bar and make everyone laugh. I'd buy boxes of champagne. I'd take a couple of my mates in there, skullduggers, they didn't like that. One of them was from Bermondsey. They weren't too struck on that. We met a couple of birds in there.

With her it was horrible. She was worse than sleeping with a woman who's like a man, and I've done that many times. It was a terrible move. I don't regret it, what's the point? But it's laughable.

CHAPTER 26

—

END OF
THE LINE

END OF THE LINE

A fter we split I went back to the cottage. The landlord was getting a bit funny, asking if I was staying or going. He'd heard rumours that I was an East End gangster and wanted me out. I never planned on staying there long-term, but I didn't have anywhere else to go at that point.

In truth, I was a mess after the split. It wasn't because of Ruth. I was regretting so many things that I'd done or not done through life, and it was all coming back to haunt me at once. True to form I dealt with it by getting drunk, coked-up, and having a few women round there late at night from the back pages of the newspapers. The neighbours didn't approve of it, but I didn't really give a fuck. On a few nights I got really pissed on vodka by myself. I drank so much a few times that I couldn't see. It was no way to live, but because I was living alone I had no one to shake me out of it so I just carried on. This went on for several weeks until I woke up one day surrounded by empty vodka bottles, used wraps of coke, and a woman who had a chin like Bruce Forsyth's. I looked at the mess that my life had become and realised it was time to up sticks.

I didn't have anywhere in particular to go so I got in touch with an old friend I knew from East London. He's very wealthy, and had a massive £15 million five-bed house in Ladbroke Grove, Notting Hill Gate. It was a house-share and he owed me a favour, so let me stay for free. I had the bottom part, and there were other people in the top. They left within weeks of me moving in, so I had the run of the place to myself. I was still selling cars and doing furniture, and was earning just about enough to feed my addictions. There wasn't much for me to do in that house apart from get out of my nut. I wasn't married any more, and my boys were off living their own lives. That meant I was alone with only my thoughts. Drink and coke were my only company. This was when my mum's death started to hit me really hard again. I couldn't stop thinking about it, and what a terrible son I'd been. To compensate for that misery I was partying hard and spending at least £1,000 a week on coke. It was a very dark place for me. Things got so bad with the coke that I thought I'd died a couple of times.

I was calling prostitutes out all the time. Like before, I had a few times where they'd stay with me all night and we wouldn't have sex. We'd just sniff gear, and they'd listen to me waffle on about all the regrets in my life. I was meeting a lot of women, too. We'd get chatting and I'd invite them back to the house. One-night stands became a common occurrence. They'd get their friends round, one thing would lead to another, and you wake up in a crowded bed. Work that one out for yourself.

The party scene was rancid, and I had a lot of unsavoury characters and leeches around me. I couldn't stand most of them, but at least they kept my mind off the reality of my life. But no matter what I did, it weighed heavily on my mind.

As well as partying in the house I started going up the West End like I used to back in my early 20s. I'd go everywhere from Mayfair to Browns – a nightclub in Holborn which my mate Angelo owned. We were in there one night when Mark Morrison walked in. He had the hump because he wanted my table. Angelo was having none of it and threw him out. He said, "Fuck off, this is for Martin." We were good friends, and I'd regularly go up there and get smashed. It was a haunt for famous people. I remember seeing Vinnie Jones and Simon Le Bon in there a few times. It was the place to go, and I spent a lot of money in there. One night I took a bloke up there called John, who I've never seen since. We ended up in a place called Tobacdoc with three birds. He went off his nut when he'd had too much powder, and did a runner. I wasn't too fussed, and ended up spending three days there with them.

I had some funny times, but the partying couldn't take away the sadness. It was always running through my mind. I kept thinking: "What's it all come to? Is it the end of the road? How far do you want to go?" I was realising that I was on the edge, and out of control.

I'd got to a stage where taking cocaine was an everyday occurrence. It didn't help that I was living in the West End, in the mix, with loads of party people. After we'd go out I'd invite everyone back to the flat to carry on the party until the early hours. It was getting to 8am and people were still sitting there doing coke. I always had terrible thoughts going through my mind. I was getting a lot of flashbacks about how successful I was as a youngster and how I threw it all away. The drug was hitting me really hard. It was working on me, and taking control of what was left of my mind. My streetwise savvy was getting chipped away.

Somehow I still kept going, just taking things day by day. I was earning a few bob. I wasn't a rich man at that stage, but I kept my head above water. The money from the cars and furniture was just enough to feed my addictions. It was a far cry from the shops, but I couldn't see that because I was so lost. Things reached a climax when I did more than £1,500 coke with a couple of other people there on a few occasions. It was out of control, and I ended up supporting other people's habits. You tend to do that when you're at that stage of taking the powder. People come round, and they're your best friend. You might get the odd one or two who put up a few bob, but that's rare. It's all like dancing and cuddling but when the party ends, the nightmare begins. That happened to me on a regular basis, more often than I had ever experienced through my addiction to the drug.

I can remember at least six occasions when I could no longer get the coke up my nose, so I was eating it with a teaspoon. I was sniffing, and nothing was going up there because it was clogged. It wasn't a nice experience, eating it on a teaspoon.

It really puts the strength of your addiction into perspective.

A couple of times there, I thought I was going to die. It came to a point when I was in the bed and my heart was beating. It was coming out of my chest. I could feel the shape of it. I was thinking "For fuck's sake. Please God, if I'm going to go, kill me now." The amount of coke I was taking meant it often took me two days just to fall asleep. My heartbeat would be racing. I would be having panic and anxiety attacks. Sitting there alone, sweating like Fred West. I was just absolutely fucked.

All I thought about was my failures in life: my relationships, my businesses, the poverty I grew up in, and the success that I threw away. There aren't many people who have done what I've done. I was a rich man very quickly, which I think might have been part of my downfall. I didn't know how to cope with the wealth. Berluti shoes, Baroni clothes, Rolex watches, Cristal and Krug champagne, Venice, holidays abroad, tit jobs like they're going out of fashion, sports cars – I've had so many Ferraris, £2m-worth of cars. I've drunk more than Elton John and Oliver Reed put together, and I probably took more coke than Pablo Escobar's sold.

It might sound fantastic, but it wasn't a great lifestyle. It might sound glorious and a high-society way of living, but at the end of it I nearly lost my life. I lost my way in life. I lost my businesses. I lost my family. And the saddest thing is I lost contact with myself. That particular house in Ladbroke Grove was a nightmare for me.

It was the end of the road. On more than one occasion I've been up there and woken up with women in my bed who I don't even know who they are. Rough as fuck. It took me days to get over it. Slowly but surely, I was losing contact with myself.

One day, things got so bad that I had to walk out of the house. I thought I was going to die. I walked to the end of the road. There was a church on the corner. I sat on the bench and passed out. I had my shirt undone. I was 18 stone, and looked dreadful. I thought I was dead. Hours later I woke up and managed to get up. Things were going through my mind: my business, my mother, my family, my upbringing, the devastation I've caused to myself, losing my way in life. It was all going through my mind at a million miles an hour. It was so much to take on board. It felt like my heart and head were going to explode. I really was at a point where I thought I was going to have a heart attack. I'd been up for three days. I remember getting back to the house. Just as I did a car pulled up with four fellas in. They were young kids, only in their 20s. They looked at me, pointed and laughed.

I've never forgotten that, to this day. It really hurt me, even though I was wasted. I've always been a proud man, trying to be smart and proper. I always had a bit of style, panache and charisma. In that moment I realised that had all gone.

I managed to get back to the gaff. How I did, I still don't know. The women were still in bed. Gear was all over the shop. There were bottles of champagne on the table. I had three people in the front room and one person in the bathroom. There was piss on the floor, and half-eaten takeaways lying around. It was a right state. I went in there and looked at them all. Even though I'd been up for three days and was out of my nut I wanted them out, that very second. I don't know what made me do it, even to this day.

I don't know if it was a stroke of luck, a miracle, God, or my mother was looking down on me, but I told myself I've got to pull myself out of this. "This is going to kill you," I said. "You've gone to the next level." I added words to the effect of "You've got to get the fuck out of here, now."

I almost dragged the women out of bed half-naked, and threw them out into the street with their knickers and bras on. There was about two grams of coke on the side. I got a note, wracked the powder up into one long line and did it all. After I'd taken it I had an explosion in my mind. I collapsed into the chair. I had all my shirt undone, with my bloated gut hanging right out. My heart was coming out of my chest. I was dripping in sweat. It makes me ill to think about it now. It was the most horrific and scary moment of my life.

I had an explosion in my head and my heart missed a beat. That had never happened to me before. I collapsed into the brown leather chair where I did the line and as I looked round I saw a picture of my mother. The thoughts that went through my mind were terrible. I was getting flashbacks to when I was a kid, my family, my kids and my father educating me. It all came as an explosion of feelings from the drug, the alcohol, the emotions, the pain, the misery, the sadness, the overwhelming nature of it all from over the past 30 years. It all hit me in one go. In one fucking line, bang, I was overcome. My head exploded and I passed out.

I woke up two days later feeling fucking terrible. I had pissed myself and was in a right state. The first thing I saw as I opened my eyes was that picture of my mother. I said to myself: "I'm alive – don't waste it." From that moment onwards, that explosion, the feelings, the misery, the sadness, the journey – doing that one line probably saved my life. That explosion, that kickback and my heart missing a beat – I woke up and saw the picture that saved my life. That was the last time I ever took coke.

When I woke up I went for a walk out of the house. I got out of breath just walking, and I thought "This is pathetic." I was never a man into fitness but I thought to myself, I can go one of two ways. I can either carry on and end up in the morgue, or I can turn my life around. At that time, I thought I was dead as a person. Martin was a character with strong willpower. He's driving his life, he's ambitious and he dreams of more. But his dreams have been killed, stone-cold dead.

But I was still walking. So I thought, I'll start from scratch, like I did when I was a kid. I'll come through the ranks from poverty and distress. I'm in the ghetto, in the slums of East London, and I'm starting again. I thought, I'll start another journey, to get myself free from the drug.

When I was walking about I was thinking, why am I alive? There must be a reason for it. Either my mum is looking down on me, or it's unexplainable. I was mentally dead. My mind was shot to bits. All my courage and my outlook and drive and willpower, and the character that I was and always have been, were dead. My character was stolen from me, and I had to get it back.

I thought, let's try and put something in place. It took me six weeks just to get clean of the drug. It will take you three months to get clean of the drug if you're a heavy user. After that, I felt like a different person. I couldn't believe it myself.

I wasn't in shape at this stage. I'd been doing a bit of fitness training. It was a weird feeling to start again, after being away from it for three months.

I disconnected from more than 500 people. I told people not to contact me whatsoever. I told everyone. I said, "Don't contact me, don't send anyone round, don't come anywhere near me, it'll be best for your own good to stay away from me." Most did what I told them. One or two didn't, and they were told in a very abrupt manner to leave immediately. I lost 500 'friends', maybe more. I knew a lot of people, from here to America. From pubs, wine bars, buying coke, sniffing coke and going round their houses. You come across a lot of characters. Most of them are liars and pricks, cheats, wafflers, and bullshitters.

Most of them aren't genuine people. Genuine people won't go into someone's house, do coke and talk bollocks. They've got a problem. If people ask me what was my problem, why did I do it, I'll tell them. It's an avenue to escape. It's an avenue to shove shit up your nose, talk bollocks and come out of my shell, tell stories that aren't real.

After a month in Notting Hill I eventually moved back to my dad's and started from scratch, building and building. Every day you get stronger.

At the start I couldn't even get up. I was 19 stone and had a 42 waist. I was in a horrendous, shameful, sad state of mind and physical appearance. I was shot to bits. To pick up the pieces from that, after what I went through and lost, was an incredible achievement. By the end I couldn't even do my shoelaces up. I couldn't even move. I was fucked. I had three chins and a red, swollen face. I was dead inside, and had no ambition. I had to battle onwards from that moment, tooth and nail, by myself, with no help. I saw a doctor about it briefly, but I had to walk out. Doctors couldn't help me. I used my own motivation.

What kept my going was that I've always known deep down that I'm a good fella, and a very strong character. I'd got caught in the crossfire, and couldn't get away from it. I say to people, I got kidnapped and it nearly killed me. But I battled like a gladiator to get back. I used to say to myself: "You've got to drag yourself out of this." In that house I had about 5 per cent of my streetwise savvy left. Maybe less. There was a very small drip left. No one would give me any help. I wasn't looking for any. I wasn't going to explain my downfall to anyone, because they're not going to believe you. They're going to laugh at you. Run you down, take the piss. I've done it myself. When I was at my father's, I'd lock myself away and do my training myself. Press-ups, running, walking.

I kept myself away from everyone, including my family. I saw my boys, but I didn't talk to anyone for about 18 months. I fucking battled to get clean. I went into an almost recluse mode to rebuild myself into the character that I was at day one. It was the only way I could do it. How could I go out for a beer? I knew what was going to happen. So I stayed in. I managed to do it. My dad was starting to help me. I was starting to eat healthily. I couldn't explain to anyone what was going through my mind.

What a dreadful state of mind I was in. Flashbacks were still coming to me on a nightly basis. But from that moment onwards, if anyone mentions the word 'cocaine' to me, it just reminds me of that explosion. That's what made me stop. Having that two grams in one hit is very dangerous. My heart rate went up to 800mph. That experience was horrible. I'd rather fight four doormen. The feeling I got was a massive rush of emotion.

The memories came to me so quickly. I remember being a young kid, playing golf. My life flashed by me at turbo speed. I remember buying my first Ferrari with a tear in my eye. There isn't a word in the English language that could describe the misery and pain that line caused me. But did it save my life?

I don't want to praise the drug, or anyone who says the

name, but it highlighted that I needed to change to stay alive. I'd been given a life sentence, and I'd just been let off. I had loads of warnings before that, but I never took any notice. That line was a very sad moment. It made me realise the memories of my mother, of friends that I'd lost, the misery that I'd caused myself and the connection I'd lost with myself, the connection I'd lost with my childhood and my principles and values. To end up in that condition for a man who had come from very meagre surroundings is a very sad thing, because I had always classed myself as a very sharp fella. I still do, even today.

I lost so much time. Cocaine robbed me of 30 years. Now I cherish time. When I wake up, even if I've got a toothache I cherish my time. When people say "I had a late one last night" I say, "Listen, I was partying for 30 years. Don't talk to me about late ones." My addiction has taken my wealth, which is immaterial, and also taken a lot of time that I could have spent with my family on my own.

I've lost valuable time, and memories that can't be replaced, because the addiction takes everything from you. It takes your feelings, your emotions, and the way you act as a person. It replaces those things with evil, stress, sadness, panic attacks and poverty. The list is endless. Anyone that says any different is lying. I'm an entrepreneur of the drug, and I can tell you just by looking at it if it's any good. That's nothing to boast about. I know it back to front, what it does, what it doesn't do. How long it lasts, when it wears off, the sexual feelings it gives you, the depression, your poverty feelings, your overall mindset.

I can tell you from the moment you put it on the worktop and cut it what is going to happen to you. Every character on the entire planet will go through the same protocol: misery, sadness, drama, depression. It's terrible. Anyone who says they've had a couple of lines of coke and they're buzzing is talking bollocks. You're buzzing for ten seconds after you have that first line. As it goes on it wears off, then the real buzz sets in. It's called misery.

I haven't slept for 30 years plus. Even to this day, I wake up at 2am and then 5am. Sleep deprivation was one thing I couldn't get back. I'm in bed by 8pm, up at 2am, up at 4am. I'd pay anything to go to bed at 9pm and get up at 7am. I just don't sleep. I've lost so many hours in 30 years of partying that my clock's all over the place. I do not sleep.

I've always been a very heavy thinker. Even as a young kid, I'd think about things at a million miles an hour. I was always a busy bee. The long-term effects are repairable. Physically, I'm fine and stable. If you asked me if there are any side effects and long-term damage I'd say sleep deprivation, and horror stories that you can't ever forget. You have to live with that. The worst one is regret, and that isn't ever going to be repaired.

Cold turkey hasn't got anything on what I went through. I went through hell, and I did it all by myself. I didn't speak to anyone for 18 months when I was rebuilding. I spoke to my sons, but I kept things tight. My family still ask me why I did it. I said I had to do it. I'm very distant from them now. I saw my mother go down to four stone, I lost two very close friends and my brother-in-law, I lost my business and my wealth that I had worked so hard for as a kid. My dreams were shattered.

It was self-inflicted, and it lasted for 30 years. I was only given a one-way ticket. For me to get a return and come back – I made that myself. I never purchased it. I had to manufacture it. I did that with willpower, determination not to let myself down, and thoughts of my mother. I wasn't going to be beaten.

That explosion I had was a wake-up call. I was dead in the mind, but my body was still alive. My life was 50/50, so I had to drag that other 50 per cent back. And the rest is history.

THE SIX-WEEK GET CLEAN PLAN

WEEK ONE

FITNESS

DAY 1

Early morning: 15 minutes brisk walk. Then 2 press-ups, repeat 3 times. Do these slow and controlled with a straight back, feet together, hands shoulder-width apart. Running on the spot for one minute, repeat 3 times with one-minute rest between each. 4 star jumps, repeat twice. Finish off with 5 minutes of basic stretching. Always keep hydrated with water.

Early evening: 10 minutes of light jogging. Then 2 sit-ups, slow and controlled. Repeat 5 times. 5 air squats. When doing squats go down as far as you can in your comfort zone. If you can't do a squat, get a chair and sit down and stand. Practise this until you get the technique right to do a squat without a chair. Finish off with 5 minutes basic stretching.

DAY 2

Early morning: 10-minute walk at a good pace. Rest for 5 minutes, repeat again. Total 20 minutes. Finish off with a good 10-minute stretch.

Early evening: Put a CD of music of your choice for no longer than 10 minutes for mini workout. Consists of running on the spot for one minute then 2 press-ups and repeat, running on the spot one minute. Then do 2 press-ups, 4 sit-ups, rest one minute. Repeat running on the spot one minute, 3 press-ups, running on the spot one minute, 3 press-ups. Finish off with as many press-ups as you can physically do. Please take note, this mini workout should not exceed 10–12 minutes to complete. Finish off with basic 5-minute slow stretch.

DAY 3

Early morning: 30 minutes swimming at your local pool. If you can't swim, option two: purchase a mountain bike and go for a 25-minute bike ride on a flat surface.Early evening: 10 minutes of basic stretching.

DAY 4

Early morning: no training.

Early evening: 25 minutes of jogging at a steady pace. Finish off with 5 minutes of basic stretching.

DAY 5

Rest day.

DAY 6

Very early start, around 6.30am: 10-minute walk at a fast pace. 10 squats, nice and slow. Use a chair if necessary. Finish off with 10 slow sit-ups.

Mid-afternoon (around 4ish): 15 minutes of jogging at a nice steady pace. Finish off with 5 star jumps. Do some stretching. Always keep hydrated.

DAY 7

No training early morning.

Around 6.30pm, mini workout consists of:

- 5 x 2 press-ups

- Running on spot for 2 minutes, no rest

- 6 squats using chair if necessary

- Out the door, 10 minutes of walking at a rapid pace. Workout complete.

NUTRITION

DAY 1

Breakfast: small bowl of porridge oats, add water or almond Alpro milk. No sugar, just a small amount of honey. 2 slices of wholemeal toast, no butter, 2 boiled eggs. Black coffee if required or any form of herbal tea.

Mid-morning snack: small pot of Greek yogurt with blueberries or any one piece of fruit. Take note, for this nutrition plan to work you will need to drink at least 3 litres of bottled water per day.

Lunch: 1 small cooked chicken breast, half a bag of brown rice, along with a small serving of broccoli or carrots.

Mid-afternoon snack: a small handful of cashew or almond nuts along with a healthy protein bar or a protein shake.

Evening meal: one small sweet potato mixed with tuna and sweetcorn (tuna in spring water), one piece of brown pitta bread, toasted.

Late-night snack if required, a small protein shake or a small serving of frozen fruit with some Greek yogurt.

DAY 2

Breakfast: 3 x Protein Weetabix with almond Alpro milk and a dash of honey to taste. Small serving of mushrooms along with scrambled eggs (2 eggs only), no bread at all. Small glass of cranberry / orange juice. Black coffee if required or herbal tea.

Mid-morning snack: one tin of tuna in spring water or 1 small chicken breast, nothing to go with it.

Lunch: 1 small serving of fresh salad only along with a very small bowl of brown pasta, no sauce.

No mid-afternoon snack, just keep hydrated.

Evening meal: any white fish with mixed vegetables only.

Late-night snack: if required, a banana along with 2 Kallo rice cakes.

DAY 3

Breakfast: 2 slices of brown toast with crunchy peanut butter, a large protein shake or a fresh-fruit smoothie.

Mid-morning snack: small portion of grapes along with two Kallo rice cakes.

Lunch: 3 x slices of cooked carvery beef, one small sweet potato with cherry tomatoes on the vine, no dressing or sauces.

Mid-afternoon snack: if required, avocado, sliced, with one Ryvita along with a small handful of cashew or almond nuts.

Evening meal: one small sirloin steak with cauliflower and broccoli.

Late-night snack: if required, a very small bowl of porridge oats with water or almond Alpro milk, no honey.

DAY 4

Breakfast: Greek yogurt along with fresh fruit, one small croissant and small glass of cranberry juice. Black coffee or herbal tea.

Mid-morning snack: two boiled eggs along with around 8 to 10 cashew nuts.

Lunch: small chicken salad along with small protein shake.

Mid-afternoon snack if required, one protein bar or one fruit and nut flapjack.

Evening meal: Lean mince with mixed vegetables, small portion.

No late-night snacks, allow yourself a Horlicks with water to sleep well.

DAY 5

Breakfast: 2 slices of wholemeal toast, small serving of smoked salmon scrambled eggs (2 eggs only). Fresh orange or cranberry juice. Black coffee or herbal tea.

Mid-morning snack: one banana with two Kallo rice cakes.

Lunch: turkey breast, cooked, half a bag of brown rice with spinach.

Mid-afternoon snack: if required, protein bar or small bag of dry roasted peanuts.

Evening meal: any white fish with a large portion of mixed vegetables.

Late-night snack: Greek yogurt along with fresh blueberries, small serving only. Take note, remember to consume at least 3 litres of bottled water a day – this is very important.

DAY 6

Breakfast: grilled tomatoes, two poached eggs, one slice of brown wholemeal toast, no butter. Black coffee or herbal tea.

Mid-morning snack: fresh-fruit smoothie, home-made or fresh-fruit mango or pineapple.

Lunch: one small jacket potato along with baked beans, half a tin, making sure you drain the juice. Small side salad if required.

No mid-afternoon snack, just water.

Evening meal: two 100% steakburgers, peas, carrots and sweetcorn, no potatoes or rice.

Late-night snack: if required, any one piece of fruit or very small protein shake.

DAY 7

Breakfast: 3 x Protein Weetabix with a dash of honey and almond milk, or 2 x boiled eggs with two slices of brown toast, no butter. Fresh orange/cranberry juice. Black coffee or herbal tea.

Mid-morning snack: one small chicken breast or two slices of cooked turkey breast, along with a handful of almond nuts.

Lunch: 1 x large chicken breast, small sweet potato with fresh leeks.

Mid-afternoon snack: a protein shake or a fresh-fruit smoothie.

Evening meal: a small ham salad.

No late-night snack, just water with sliced lemon.

MOTIVATION

DAY 1

1. Immediately change your mobile phone number.

2. Disconnect from your circle of friends who use cocaine.

3. Accept that you have an addiction.

4. Remember you, and only you, are the key to getting clean.

5. Drastic actions need to be put in place immediately.

6. You must now take control of your life.

7. Plant this seed deep inside your head: cocaine has taken everything from you.

8. Cocaine is not the power. Remember that you are the power.

9. Today's mindset is as folllows:

Think about all the money you have wasted on the drug.

Think about how rough you feel after using the drug.

10. Remember other side-effects you currently suffer from:

- Panic attacks
- Depression
- Sadness

EMOTIONAL PROBLEMS

- Racing heartbeat
- Mood swings
- Unhealthy diet
- Health deterioration
- Relationship problems
- Financial ruin
- Distant family,
- and worst of all,
- Losing your pride and personality.

11. Note and remember number 10 on the list. All those side-effects you are actually paying for out of your hard-earned money. You should feel like a complete fool.

12. Now you can start to piece your life back together by using the list above to make you battle tooth and nail to get clean from the drug.

13. Every time you get a craving for the drug, use the list as your defence mindset and body armour.

DAY 2

Put these thoughts deep inside your mind:

- Happiness
- Healthy lifestyle
- Motivation
- Clean eating
- Very focused
- Unstoppable
- Positive decisions
- Strong mindset
- Enjoying life
- Striving for success
- Strong relationships
- Feeling confident
- Very streetwise
- Very sharp
- Powerful
- Proud
- Successful.

If you need to obtain this unique set of skills, make the change: stop using the drug, and start living the dream.

Read this paragraph every single day during your six-week plan.

DAY 3

Remember the amount of cash you think you have spent on cocaine all the time you have been hooked on the drug. Write the amount down on an A4 piece of paper using a marker pen. Make copies of that piece of paper and place one in each room, on the wall, so every time you walk into the room that amount hits you full-on and makes you physically sick.

You may question my unique methods of getting clean from the drug, but after 30 years as a very heavy user of cocaine, these methods worked for me. The aim being: trying to build a mindset that eventually you will despise cocaine. I used all the bad points about cocaine to my advantage, to pull myself out of the addiction and turn those negative thoughts into a very strong, powerful mindset. A strong mindset will always overcome any addiction, full stop.

DAY 4

Find two pictures of your parents when they were young. Take pictures of them on your mobile phone and use that as your screen saver. Make a point of looking at those pictures as many times as you can throughout your day, and then take a moment to remember that these two special people brought you into the world, and you repaid them by sniffing cocaine with undesirable people in surroundings that are shameful, and worst of all, you are completely off your mind on the drug.

How do you think they would feel if they knew these circumstances about the child they brought into the world?

They would feel:

- Devastated
- Heartbroken

- Shocked.

Be hard on yourself, and once again use these tragic thoughts to pull yourself together and get clean from the drug.

Keep building your strength.

Take something good from something dreadful.

DAY 5

If necessary, move to a new location and change jobs. It sounds harsh, but these steps need to be taken. A job is replaceable. Your health and family are not. New surroundings can be a great leap forward from drug addiction. We all know that cocaine can be purchased in any area, but on the good side, if you do pack up ship and move to a new location it will be unlikely that you have many contacts there.

You must be willing to take extraordinary decisions to narrow down and shut as many doors as you can to stop yourself purchasing the drug. Don't make excuses, don't lie to yourself. The sooner you put these moves in place, the sooner you will give yourself a chance to repair your life. The damage is done, but once again try and draw something good from these extreme decisions, and praise yourself for accepting that you need to act swiftly.

Under no circumstances worry about what other people say or how they judge your unusual behaviour. Your life and future lie in your hands. Rely on no one or anything else to help you repair your life from this horrible drug.

DAY 6

Mindset for today – stay positive, fight the powder.

Plant this in your mind: 5 days clean already!!! Make no mistake, this 6-week plan is not easy, because for the first three weeks it will seem like you are running yourself down, but in reality you are facing up to the truth.

So, key points for today: Your achievement of 5 days clean should be a good source of motivation for you in the early stages of getting clean. Now, imagine how strong you will be in 3 weeks.

3 major points to remember:

- You are the power, not the cocaine

- You are now in the driving seat and not the passenger seat

- The road ahead from now on is going to be straight, with no turnings and no stop-off points.

DAY 7

Today is about recharging your mind and looking forward to attacking your addiction with the correct ingredients and tools to overcome the horrible white powder.

Embrace your first week of being clean, taking on board that you are strong, clear-headed, and in a position to put an end to this terrible addiction that has stolen and robbed you of time and happiness that belongs to you.

Remember this: There is no answer at the end of a line of cocaine, apart from misery. Focus on the thought that your powerful determination will give you back what truly belongs to yourself. Being clean from the drug costs nothing apart from your will-power and your self-pride. Using the drug could cost you your life.

WEEK TWO

FITNESS

DAY 1

Early morning: 15 minutes jogging at steady pace followed by 3 press-ups repeat 5 times. 3 squats repeated 5 times, using chair if needed. Finish off running on the spot, rapid pace. Remember to keep hydrated.

Early evening: mini workout, 2 sets of 10 sit-ups. Out the door, 10 minutes walking at a rapid pace, finish off with as many squats as possible. Finish with basic stretching.

DAY 2

Early morning: swimming pool, as many lengths as possible at a slow pace, or 30-minute bike ride at steady pace.

Early evening: 20-minute walk, slow-pace workout. Keep hydrated.

DAY 3

Rest day / optional training.

Early morning: 10 minutes skipping or 2-minute sprints with 2-minute rest. Repeat 5 times.

Evening: 15 minutes of basic stretching.

DAY 4

Early morning: 20 squats, using chair if necessary. As many sit-ups as possible. Finish off with 10 minutes dancing to your favourite tunes in the comfort of your home.

Evening: as many press-ups as you can, no rest. Then sit-ups, as many as you can, no rest.

DAY 5

Early morning: sprints for one minute and then perform 2 press-ups. Repeat 5 times. Finish off with a 15-minute steady-pace walk.

Evening: 15 minutes stretching.

DAY 6

Rest day.

DAY 7

Early morning: mini workout: 15-minute jog, good pace, then 15 air squats. 5 press-ups, repeat 3 times. 5 sets of 5 star jumps, finish off with 6 sit-ups, repeat 5 times.

Evening: rest.

NUTRITION

DAY 1

Breakfast: porridge oats with water or almond Alpro milk, add honey to taste. 2 slices of wholemeal toast with crunchy peanut butter. Small protein shake, black coffee or herbal tea.

Mid-morning snack: one banana, 2 x rice cakes.

Lunch: small chicken salad, no dressing. Small glass of fresh orange or cranberry juice.

Mid-afternoon snack: protein bar or small handful of almond and cashew nuts.

Evening meal: small bowl of brown pasta with tuna and sweetcorn, no sauce.

Late-night snack: small serving of Greek yogurt and blueberries.

DAY 2

Breakfast: protein Weetabix with almond milk, slice of banana and honey to taste. 2 boiled eggs, one slice of wholemeal toast, no butter. Black coffee or herbal tea.

No mid-morning snack, just keep hydrated.

Lunch: small chicken breast, half a bag of brown rice.

Mid-afternoon snack: one small tin of tuna in spring water or one piece of fruit

Evening meal: large portion of mixed vegetables along with protein shake and a bottle of water. Try and drink 3 litres of water a day.

Late-night snack: protein bar, or a small bowl of mixed fruit.

DAY 3

Breakfast: scrambled eggs (only 2 eggs), grilled tomatoes, no bread. Black coffee or herbal tea.

Mid-morning snack: small handful of almond or cashew nuts.

Lunch: 3 x slices of turkey breast, cooked, with small sweet potato and spinach.

Mid-afternoon snack: a fruit and nut oatmeal flapjack.

Evening meal: one small sirloin steak with broccoli and cauliflower. No potatoes or rice. Small glass of fresh orange or cranberry juice.

Late-night snack: 2 x rice cakes with fresh fruit jam.

DAY 4

Breakfast: Greek yogurt with mixed frozen fruit, small protein shake or home-made smoothie. Black coffee or herbal tea.

Mid-morning snack: one small chicken breast or small tin of tuna in spring water.

Lunch: 2 x boiled eggs with a green salad.

No mid-afternoon snack: keep hydrated with bottled water.

Evening meal: any piece of white fish, half bag of brown rice, peas and carrots.

Late-night snack: a small portion of grapes.

DAY 5

Breakfast: porridge oats with water or almond Alpro milk. Protein shake or fresh-fruit smoothie, home-made, one banana.

No mid-morning snack.

Lunch: 3 slices carvery roast beef, one small jacket potato, no butter or dressing. Glass of cranberry or orange juice, fresh only.

Mid-afternoon snack: a small bag of dry roasted peanuts. Keep hydrated.

Evening meal: 2 x 100% steakburgers, small portion of sweet-potato fries, along with large portion of mixed vegetables.

Late-night snack: small Greek yogurt with fresh frozen fruit.

DAY 6

Breakfast: small portion of mushrooms, 4 x poached eggs, one toasted granary roll, no butter. Black coffee or herbal tea.

Mid-morning snack: protein shake with an apple.

Lunch: smoked mackerel, small portion of vegetable rice, no bread.

Mid-afternoon snack: 2 x rice cakes with crunchy peanut butter.

Always keep hydrated.

Evening meal: small penne pasta with ham and mixed side salad. One Ryvita.

Late-night snack: home-made smoothie of your choice.

DAY 7

Breakfast: a glass of fresh orange or cranberry juice. One plain croissant with fresh fruit jam, 2 x bananas. Black coffee or herbal tea.

Mid-morning snack: mango or fresh pineapple.

Lunch: one large chicken breast, swede, mashed potato, large portion of broccoli. Keep hydrated.

Mid-afternoon snack: fruit and nut flapjack bar or 12 almond nuts.

Evening meal: small portion of mixed seafood, stir fried. Glass of cranberry juice.

Late-night snack: Horlicks, just add water.

MOTIVATION

DAY 1
Mindset

Focus once again on how rough you would always feel after using the drug, and also remember how bad your judgement was in all aspects of life when using the drug. How it affects your relationships, business, finances, and everyday simple chores become a problem. Two main points to remember when you're on the drug:

1. Your mindset is out of your control.

2. You begin to lie to yourself and convince yourself that you are in control, but in reality you are not.

DAY 2

Remember, today all your hard-earned wages and cash are being given to a drug dealer to make you feel depressed, with low mood and no self-esteem. Everything becomes a problem, and the worst thing is that you are actually paying someone to feel like this.

You worked to try and provide a better standard of living for you and your family, but now the drug has crept in and is also in charge of your finances.

Make no mistake about it whatsoever, your life is no longer your own. You have a problem which won't go away by itself.

Don't kid yourself, getting clean from the powder is a full-time job. It needs to be dealt with quickly and swiftly before you are completely out of control of your life.

DAY 3

A main point to remember when trying to get clean from cocaine: No one is going to offer you help. Many people will give you verbal advice, which is of no use whatsoever because they have not experienced the drug and the addiction that you are going through. When I was trying to get clean off the drug, I eventually realised that the only person you can turn to for advice, motivation and hope is yourself. So in layman's terms, you must become your own mentor, and rely upon no one apart from yourself. If you make mistakes along your journey on recovering from the drug you only have yourself to blame – but on a good note, you can build strong defences by learning from your mistakes, recognising them quickly, and nipping them in the bud.

DAY 4

One of my main points that got me through my journey as an addict was to replace the cocaine addiction with something I enjoyed, which turned out to be fitness. In the very early stages getting of clean from the drug I found that boredom was a dangerous word, and a dangerous place to be. The reason being that the cravings can kick in severely. As an example, when the cravings kick in, which they will, make sure that you have something in place immediately to take your mind off the drug, such as training, cooking, or a hobby of your choice.

DAY 5

In the early part of my journey, I began to think that the addiction was an easy thing to put a stop to. But let me tell you, you will have a rude awakening because cocaine is a very crafty drug. It will sneak up on you when you are at your lowest point, and attack you full-on to enhance your craving for using the drug. My mindset was as follows: I began to think back on a regular basis to when I was a clean-living young man with no addiction issues; it is almost like going back in time to your childhood and realising you have taken the wrong route in life. You may question my unusual tactics for getting clean from the drug, but what I tried to do repeatedly was to build up a strong body armour to prevent myself in any way possible from using the drug again.

DAY 6

What worked for me may sound strange. On my journey getting clean from the drug, I always gave myself a very tough time. Reasons for this are as follows: I knew I was a good man deep down inside. I knew that I could overcome this addiction. Being positive and powerful in your mind, no matter how low you are or how bad your addiction is, there is always a way out. The reasons why I always gave myself a hard time were to understand that this drug was not going to disappear overnight. It needed my full attention at all times to overcome it. The point is, once again, take something good out of something dreadful, and use it to your advantage.

DAY 7

Always remember that cocaine has stolen quality time from you and your family. It can be replaced by you dealing with your addiction, putting drastic steps in place to get clean from the drug. For example moving house, seeking new employment elsewhere, obviously disconnecting from bad company, if need be even separating from your partner if they are a heavy user of the drug as well. You may shed a tear, but in the long run you will be the winner.

WEEK THREE

FITNESS

DAY 1

Early morning: 15 minutes jogging at a steady pace followed by 3 press-ups, repeat 5 times. 3 squats repeated 5 times, using chair if needed. Finish off running on the spot, rapid pace. Keep hydrated.

Early evening: mini workout: 20 sit-ups, 10 x 2 reps. Then out the door, 10 minutes walking at a rapid pace, finish off with as many squats as possible. Finish with 10 minutes basic stretching.

DAY 2
Early morning: 25-minute jog. Keep hydrated.

Early evening: 10 minutes dancing to music of your choice. Finish off with as many sit-ups as possible.

DAY 3
Early morning: 5 press-ups, repeated four times. 3 minutes running on the spot. 10 x leg raisers. Finish off with 5-minute stretch.

Evening: rest.

DAY 4
Early morning: 40-minute walk, steady pace, finish off with 10-minute stretch.

Evening: 20 air squats, 5 sit-ups, repeat 5 times. 10 leg raises.

DAY 5
Early morning: speed walk 10 minutes, finish off with 20 press-ups, sets of 5, slow.

Evening: 15 minutes basic stretching.

DAY 6
Early morning: 20 press-ups, 5 minutes sprinting, 10 minutes skipping. 25 Leg raisers, 10 minutes stretching.

Evening: rest.

DAY 7

Mid-afternoon: nice slow bike ride, 30 minutes, or slow walk, 30 minutes. Finish off with 5 minutes stretching.

NUTRITION

DAY 1

Breakfast: 2 boiled eggs on granary toast, no butter. One banana and a small protein shake

No mid-morning snack. Keep hydrated.

Lunch: small chicken salad with cranberry or orange juice. Black coffee or herbal tea.

Mid-afternoon snack: protein shake.

Evening meal: brown pasta with tuna and sweetcorn, no dressing.

Late-night snack: frozen fruit with Greek yogurt.

DAY 2

Breakfast: porridge oats with sliced banana or Greek yogurt. One piece of fruit. Black coffee or herbal tea.

Mid-morning snack: 2 x rice cakes with 100% fresh-fruit jam.
Lunch: small sweet potato, one small chicken breast, no dressing.

Mid-afternoon snack: small packet of dry roasted peanuts or fresh-fruit smoothie.

Evening meal: small sirloin steak, half a packet of brown rice.

Late-night snack: apple or orange.

DAY 3

Breakfast: 3 scrambled eggs, mix in some mushrooms and lean grilled bacon. Fresh orange or cranberry juice. Black coffee or herbal tea. Drink 3 litres of water to keep hydrated.

Mid-morning snack: banana.

Lunch: 3 x slices of turkey breast with plum tomatoes, iceberg lettuce and half a bag of brown rice. If you don't like turkey have ham, chicken or beef, but don't overload.

Evening meal: lean minced meat with vegetables, large serving.

No late-night snack.

DAY 4

Breakfast: 3 x Weetabix with almond Alpro milk with a dash of honey.

Mid-morning snack: one banana, one protein shake and a small handful of cashew nuts.

Lunch: small bowl of pasta and sweetcorn and one chicken breast. Large glass of water with a slice of lemon. Allow yourself two squares of 80% dark chocolate.

Mid-afternoon snack: Greek yogurt with honey and banana, or a protein bar or small protein shake.

Evening meal: fresh prawn stir-fry and a side salad.

No late-night snack.

DAY 5

Breakfast: porridge and fruit.

Mid-morning snack: 2 slices of brown wholemeal toast and 2 boiled eggs with black coffee, herbal tea or water.

Lunch: small jacket potato with beans and a granary roll with no butter.

No mid-afternoon snack.

Evening meal: 100% beefburger with mixed vegetables.
Dessert: small serving of cheesecake.

Late-night snack: fruit of your choice.

DAY 6

Breakfast: one slice of toast with honey and banana.

Mid-morning snack: protein shake and a handful of walnuts.

Lunch: chicken salad and Ryvita.

Mid-afternoon snack: water.

Evening: tuna salad with brown rice.

Late-night snack: Horlicks.

DAY 7

Breakfast: bowl of mixed fruit and Greek yogurt.

Mid-morning snack: small protein shake.

Lunch: small bowl of brown pasta and a small serving of 100% lean mince with a glass of water.

Mid-afternoon snack: fresh-fruit smoothie or a protein shake.

Evening meal: one breast of chicken with large portion of vegetables.

Late-night snack: 2 rice cakes with crunchy peanut butter.

MOTIVATION

DAY 1

Mindset for today is very simple: be hard on yourself with all the money you've spend on cocaine. Drum it into your head, you're paying this money to get a buzz, but in reality it was slowly ruining your life and turning you into someone else – a horrible person who didn't care about anyone but the powder. Make that thought hit you hard so you can understand that you were spending money to feel like shit and act like a fool. It may be a strange way to get clean from the drug, but it worked for me. The reason being, I built up such a hatred for the drug that I started to get angry when I even heard the word cocaine. That helped me rebuild my mind and grow and be strong to defend myself against it.

DAY 2

Don't forget to look at the pieces of paper you've posted around the house, showing the amount of money you've spent on cocaine. Look at them every day during your 6-week journey. You should now slowly be feeling a bit better, even though it always seems like you're running yourself down. I also got that feeling. Things will get a lot better as time goes on, and you'll see changes come all at once. It's a great feeling, better than any coke, and it's all your own work, and it's your positive mindset getting you there.

DAY 3

Today is about knowing your worth, and that means you're not a two-bob coke-head. Knowing my worth helped me rebuild my mind very quickly, and it will also make you very hungry to get back on track. Think about everyday living, for example cleaning

263

your house, paying your bills on time, putting plans in place for a better life, and making the best of what you have.

DAY 4

All day today, remember how far you've come already. Feel proud, but also remember you'll get a backlash. Soon you'll be overcome by massive cravings for cocaine. That is part of the journey, so be ready for it because it will happen. Focus is the key for today. It's not easy, but if you can get outside and have a refreshing walk it will make you feel better.

DAY 5

Make a point of doing stuff you haven't done for ages. For example, get rid of old clothes, or go and see an old friend. Don't focus your thoughts and feelings on the past, just live a normal day, like a clean person would live.

DAY 6

Focus on family. Remember they've always been there for you from day one. Don't focus on the dramas of life, just enjoy it. In your mind the battle isn't over yet. If you keep going, you can win it.

Focus on getting clean, nothing else matters. Focus on your new mindset, but begin to understand your feelings and know your place in life.

DAY 7

You're halfway there! WOW! Spend most of the day out enjoying yourself, but remember – no drink or drugs. Congratulate yourself on how far you've come, but remember you've got a long way to go.

WEEK FOUR

FITNESS

DAY 1

Early morning: 45-minute jog followed by 25 sit-ups and 25 press-ups, no rest or break. Finish off with 10 minutes of star jumps.

Early evening: 1-hour walk.

DAY 2

Early morning: 25-minute jog. Then 4 x 10 sit-ups and 4 x 5 sets of slow press-ups. Finish off with 5 air squats, repeat 4 times.

Early evening: stretching and sit-ups, as many as you can.

DAY 3

Rest day.

DAY 4

Early morning: 1 hour walking at a good pace, then as many squats as you can do. Dancing for 10 minutes to music of your choice.

Evening: training: 10 minutes skipping.

DAY 5

Early morning: 30-minute jog, good pace. 10 press-ups, repeat 5 times, followed by 10 minutes stretching.

Early evening: 10 minutes skipping.

DAY 6

Early morning: mini workout: Go to a local park. Do 2-minute sprints, repeat 5 times. Then 10 press-ups, repeat 5 times.

Finish with 10 minutes skipping and walk back home.

Evening: rest.

DAY 7

Early morning: light jog around the park.

Evening: rest.

NUTRITION

DAY 1

Breakfast: one banana, large protein shake. Black coffee or herbal tea.

Mid-morning snack: 2 x rice cakes with fresh-fruit jam. Water and herbal tea.

Lunch: 2 pieces of cooked chicken breast with veg, dry roasted peanuts. Black coffee.

Mid-afternoon snack: banana with some water.

Evening meal: any white fish of your choice with veg and no dressing.

Late-night snack: frozen fruit with Greek yogurt.

DAY 2

Breakfast: 3 x scrambled eggs with vine tomatoes and mushrooms.

Mid-morning snack: banana and protein bar.

Lunch: small sweet potato, one small chicken breast with green-leaf mixed salad. Glass of juice of your choice.

Mid-afternoon snack: 2 rice cakes with a small amount of crunchy peanut butter and a small black coffee.

Evening meal: small sirloin steak, half a packet of brown rice, and a small serving of peas and carrots.

Late-night snack: apple or orange.

DAY 3

Breakfast: 2 x boiled eggs, 2 x slices of wholemeal toast. Small fresh juice and 1 litre cold water.

Mid-morning snack: piece of fruit and water.

Lunch: small portion of pasta with tuna and sweetcorn, optional brown roll with no butter. Black coffee or herbal tea.

Mid-afternoon snack: piece of fruit or protein shake.

Evening: 4 slices of carvery beef with sweet potato mash and large serving of veg. From now on only decaf black coffee.

Late-night treat: small bag of popcorn.

DAY 4

Breakfast: porridge with almond milk and a banana.

Mid-morning snack: decaf black coffee and protein shake.

Lunch: chicken breast, veg and bottle of water.

Mid-afternoon snack: piece of fruit and bottle of water.

Evening meal: egg salad with black coffee.

No late-night snack.

DAY 5

Breakfast: smoked salmon and scrambled eggs with brown wholemeal toast. No butter and a slice of lemon for the salmon. Black coffee and herbal tea.

Mid-morning snack: piece of fruit of your choice and water.

Lunch: small jacket potato with beans and a tin of tuna. Decaf black coffee.

Mid-afternoon snack: protein shake.

Evening: large sirloin steak, sweet potato fries with mushrooms and onions.

Late-night snack: Cornetto with a 99 flake.

DAY 6

Breakfast: 3 poached eggs with mushrooms, tomatoes and brown toast. Decaf black coffee.

Mid-morning snack: protein shake and a handful of walnuts.

Lunch: chicken salad and Ryvita.

Mid-afternoon snack: piece of fruit and water.

Evening: lean minced meat with mixed veg.

Late-night snack: Horlicks.

DAY 7

Breakfast: bowl of mixed fruit and Greek yogurt.

Mid-morning snack: small protein shake.

Lunch: small bowl of brown pasta with tuna and sweetcorn, no dressing. Glass of water.

Mid-afternoon snack: fresh-fruit smoothie or a protein shake.

Evening: 1 breast of chicken with large portion of vegetables.

Late-night snack: 2 x rice cakes with crunchy peanut butter.

MOTIVATION

DAY 1

Today don't think about cocaine at all. Have no bad feelings, just focus on day-to-day living. It is going to be hard but you have got to get it done, it's part of getting clean. The best way to do this is to stay busy. Your mindset will be ready for this by now. In my journey my mind was in overdrive thinking about how terrible the drug was, and I was fighting like fuck to beat off the cravings from the cocaine man. It was hell. To beat it I kept looking in the mirror to see how well I looked. I also kept on looking at the pieces of paper that said how much I had spent on gear – that was a big help.

DAY 2

Focus on your success and how far you've come. Praise yourself on your journey so far. Things are getting better as the days and weeks go by, so focus on becoming stronger and being more alive.

Things will now start to take shape, and your outlook will start to become clearer.

Slowly but surely you are getting back to yourself, and a great feeling will start to come over you. You will feel so proud!

DAY 3

Always remember to look at the pieces of paper with the amount of money you have wasted on cocaine. Look at pictures of your mum and dad, and pictures of you when you were young and clean, and recall memories of happy times. Always remember this: cocaine will ruin your life, you will have no money, family will part from you, your life will be out of control. Remember that's not happening any more, now you are fighting back.

DAY 4

If you can do one thing today, be strong. Try and block out negative thoughts, and get on with your day. I blocked out anything negative. The reason I did this was to prove to myself that I can do whatever. It was as simple as that. The feeling was almost unreal. I had tears of joy: now I am on my way to getting clean from cocaine.

DAY 5

Mindset today is going back to basics. Remember you may have fucked up hundreds of times, but understand that your journey to getting clean has enabled you to put things right. It's about facing up to your mistakes. It's a tough test, but it's what you need to do. It's always going to be very, very hard, but trust me, if you can get this done you've done 90% of your journey to getting clean.

DAY 6

Today is about telling yourself "I'm a winner". It's about overcoming anger and feeling joy, and accepting all the money and time you've wasted on the powder. Put the gear down, and move forward with your life.

DAY 7

Keep your strong mindset. Stay focused. Don't ever try and convince yourself that you are 100% clean. You're not there yet, but you've done 4 weeks and you should be unstoppable. Always look at that piece of paper showing the amount of money you've spent on cocaine. Keep that in your mind as you move forward.

WEEK FIVE

FITNESS

DAY 1

Early morning: 10 minutes jogging, rapid pace, no rest period. 20 press-ups straight. 15 air squats, no rest period. 15 sit-ups, no rest period. 5 x 5 leg raisers. 3 minutes skipping or 3 minutes star jumps, as many as you can. 10 minutes stretch, workout complete.

Early evening: 45-minute walk at a steady pace, 10 press-ups, finish with a 10-minute stretch, job done.

DAY 2

Early morning: mini workout, 4 x 10 sit-ups, 5 x 5 leg raisers, 5 burpees x 2, total 10, running on spot for 4 minutes, rapid, twice. Plank, one minute, hold, repeat 3 times. High knees, one minute, repeat 3 times. Finish off with 25 air squats, nice and slow. 10-minute basic stretch, workout complete.

Mid-afternoon: 15-minute jog, at a rapid pace if you can.

Early evening: no training, just do a slow 20-minute stretch.

DAY 3

Early morning: 30-minute bike ride or 30-minute swim, 10 minutes skipping on and off, finish off with as many sit-ups as you can.

Mid-afternoon: 1-minute walk then sprint for one minute if you can, repeat 5 times, finish off with 4 x press-ups, total 40.

Early evening: mini workout indoors, 10 x 5 sit-ups, 10 x 5 leg raisers, 10 x 5 air squats, 10 x 5 press-ups, 4 x one-minute plank workout, job done.

DAY 4
Early morning: no training.

Early evening: 10 x 4 sit-ups, 10 x 4 press-ups, 10-minute stretch, workout complete.

DAY 5
Early morning: 30 minutes of jogging, no rest, 10 x 4 leg raisers, 10 x 4 sit-ups, 10 x 4 press-ups, 5-minute stretch, job done.

Mid-afternoon: 30-minute speed walk, no rest, finish off with 10-minute stretch.

Early evening: no training, rest.

DAY 6
Early morning: no training.

Early evening: 1 hour slow jog back home, 15-minute basic stretch, workout complete.

DAY 7
Early morning: 30 leg raisers, 3 sets of ten, 30 sit-ups, 6 sets of 5, 50 press-ups, 10 sets of 5, 4 one-minute plank holds, 10 burpees, finish off by skipping as long as you can. Workout done.

Early evening: 30-minute slow jog, workout complete.

NUTRITION

DAY 1
Breakfast: porridge oats, water or almond Alpro milk, frozen fruit and a banana, protein shake, small amount of cashew nuts.

Mid-morning snack: 2 boiled eggs or small bunch of grapes or 2 plain Kallo rice cakes.

Lunch: half a bag of brown rice with mixed peppers and spring onions with chicken or turkey breast, no dressing. One small brown pitta bread. Decaf black coffee or herbal tea. Always drink 3 litres of bottled water a day.

Mid-afternoon snack: any piece of fruit or a flapjack protein bar.

Evening meal: 100% steakburgers x 2, small sweet potato with broccoli, cauliflower and peas.

Late-night snack: small portion of Greek yogurt and a dash of honey.

DAY 2

Breakfast: fresh orange or cranberry juice, granola mixed with Greek yogurt, add some honey and one banana. Decaf coffee.

Mid-morning snack: small tomato salad or a very small bowl of penne pasta with no sauce, just add red onion and pepper.

Lunch: small ham salad (ham off the bone), tomatoes, iceberg lettuce, beetroot and celery, no dressing

Mid-afternoon snack: a home-made smoothie or a protein shake and a small packet of dry roasted nuts.

Evening meal: Mediterranean vegetables, one piece of fresh salmon with a small portion of white rice, only half a bag. Water or fresh juice, no coffee.

No late-night snack.

DAY 3

Breakfast: Protein Weetabix with almond Alpro milk and a banana and some raisins. 2 x boiled eggs, one slice of toast, wholemeal, no butter.

Mid-morning snack: one small avocado on toast and salt and pepper to taste, one small black decaf coffee.

Lunch: sliced turkey breast with a small jacket potato, a side salad, tomato and onions. As always, drink 3 litres of bottled water a day.

Mid-afternoon snack: Greek yogurt with mixed frozen fruit plus one banana or two plain Kallo rice cakes with crunchy peanut butter or 100% fruit jam with a glass of fresh fruit juice.

Evening meal: a small tuna salad, no dressing, one brown roll on butter, a glass of cranberry juice.

Late-night snack: small protein shake with water.

DAY 4
Breakfast: smoked salmon on two scrambled eggs. Black coffee or herbal tea.

No mid-morning snack.

Lunch: a packed lunch: fresh cooked chicken with brown rice and peas and some fruit.

No mid-afternoon snack.

A very light evening meal: a small protein shake, or two bananas on toast and a dash of honey.

Late-night snack: Horlicks with water.

DAY 5
Breakfast: Porridge oats with a banana, other fresh fruit or a large protein shake. Black decaf coffee or herbal tea.

No mid-morning snack.

Lunch: One sweet potato, 4 x slices of turkey breast or carvery beef with a small serving of mixed veg, 2 x rice cakes. Fresh fruit juice or herbal tea.

Mid-afternoon snack: fruit and nut flapjack, small protein shake.

Evening meal: 2 large boiled eggs on toast with mushrooms, one very small sirloin steak.

No late-night snack.

DAY 6
Breakfast: Greek yogurt with mixed fruit, 3 protein Weetabix mixed in with the yogurt and fruit. One slice of brown toast. Small decaf black coffee or herbal tea.

No mid-morning snack.

Go out for lunch. Keep it clean, just a small salad of your choice.

No mid-afternoon snack.

Evening meal: Any white fish, large portion of mixed veg and one small sweet potato. Please remember to drink 3 litres of bottled water every day.

Late-night snack: Horlicks.

DAY 7
A very light breakfast: small bowl of porridge oats, honey, milk or water, 2 x bananas plus small decaf coffee, water or fresh fruit juice.

Mid-morning snack: large protein shake or fruit and nut flapjack, or small packet of dry roasted peanuts.

Late lunch: a very small avocado salad, no bread or dressing at all, three slices of fresh pineapple.

No mid-afternoon snack. Just keep hydrated.

Evening meal: 2 x chicken breasts with large portion of vegetables, no rice or potatoes.

Late-night snack: 2 x boiled eggs or a small protein shake.

MOTIVATION

DAY 1

Now we are 4 weeks ahead, so push forward more on your weaker points? WRONG – no weak points: mindset strong and on point. You should now be able to think more about getting things back on track, such as tidying up your current financial issues, and dealing with problems head-on, where before you just leave the problems to get worse.

Even put in place a surprise holiday for you and your family or partner. If you are single, go alone and unwind. I suggest you do this some time over the next 3 months, that way the money you have saved from not being on the gear will cover it nicely.

So for all of week 5 it's about putting things in place that will give you pleasure, and of course peace of mind. What I also did was not easy, but by God I learnt a lot from it.

Try this, as you are now on Week 5 of your journey. It's a real test of your mind and strength. On Day Five of this week (Friday) pay a visit to one of the many places you used to go. It may be a pub, a wine bar or social club. Stroll in there around 9.30pm on

Friday night, you will see all the same old faces, trust me. Saying "Where have you been?" and chewing your ears off. Order a glass of lemonade or orange juice, then leave. Of course you will have all of your so-called mates offering you gear, but you refuse. Just take a moment to look and listen to them all. Trust me, when you walk out of that door it will be the best feeling you have ever had. It's a priceless move on your behalf.

Back to today's mindset:

1. Think about booking a holiday2. Sort out your finances3. Put things in place that bring you pleasure.

Your mind should feel clear now, and your body cleaner. Remember how far you have come: it's a very important point. Remember your mindset plan, putting things in place that make you happy. Going to an event, booking a show, repainting a room in your house or flat, maybe do some reading, or you may just want to be normal and not be off your head. It felt strange for me to be normal. Things were so much clearer now and my direction in life became enjoyable. Remember who you are. You're in control now. Your mind is now on board, no mistakes. Always remember to keep looking at those posters all over your house showing the amount of money you spent on cocaine – very important.

DAY 2

Mindset for today: start to give your family more care and love, like helping your kids with their homework, taking more interest in their schooling. Laugh you may, but when I was off my head I never spent any quality time with my sons – shameful – or any of my family, because we all know when you're on gear your mind and feelings don't count. Show your partner some more love and affection. It's a great feeling. You know you've always wanted to, but the cocaine doesn't allow happiness, as we all know only too well. Try to understand as well that you must begin to like yourself – sounds a bit wacky, but when you're on cocaine you hate yourself terribly. Now you are 90% clean, this is the time to get back your mojo. This is very important to you, the reason being, when you're totally clean from cocaine you still need to be alert, because it's so easy to slip back into your old ways, but if you are confident in yourself and your pride is through the roof, the drug is fighting a losing battle.

Remember:

1. Getting your mojo back
2. Pride through the roof
3. 100% confident about yourself.

Remember: cocaine stole your time and took your cash. Always be very clear about that, and remind yourself how much you hate that horrible white powder.

Late-night mindset: switch off when you go to bed, and sleep with a clear head.

DAY 3
Mindset today, simple.

Try and think of one person you know that is on the gear and living a happy life. It won't happen. Now look at your set-up: healthy food, family back on track, looking sharp and on point with anything life can throw at you. The point of this mindset is simple: you now know that everything is within your reach. Plant this in your head: everything is now up for grabs – more happiness, more opportunities, more doors opened, more avenues to explore. It's a win-win situation. Keep this in your mind: you are only going forward and never going backwards, your life has changed in such a short time – amazing. Relax now for the rest of the evening.

DAY 4

Mindset for today: this is what I have done. I got a packed lunch together and drove 50 miles to a seaside town, and took my training gear with me. On arrival I went on the beach for a 30-minute run. This is great. If you're thinking, "Why drive down to the seaside during the week?" the answer is "Why, because I can." I can now do things that I want, as cocaine is not running my life – as simple as that, but what a feeling it was sitting there having my packed lunch, watching time go by and enjoying every minute of it. Take note, you don't have to drive to the seaside, but just do something out of the blue because you can. Try it – it's a great feeling, trust me. Bed by 9.30pm. Enjoy the moment. I remember it well! Tears of joy – what a moment!

DAY 5

Mindset is all about tonight, as we said in Day One.

It's all about tonight – a big test of strong will-power for yourself. Around 9.30 in the evening you set out to do a big challenge for yourself. I did! On the way home, around 10.30pm, I was in tears – fucking hell, I'd done it. I walked away from fools and walked away from cocaine. I slept like never before: speechless, head held high.

DAY 6

Mindset today: put cocaine away, just take in your victory from last night, having a nice normal Saturday, eg. do some shopping for your final week – clean food only. Treat today like a rest day from your mindset. Chill, relax, enjoy your time, from the moment you wake up to the moment you go to bed. Bed around 9.30pm, feeling great, WOW!

DAY 7

Your mindset today is back in gear. You must get it as solid as you can in your mind, as the next week is going to be the test of your life, so today just store up what you've learnt so far. Put it all in your mind. I know it's a lot to remember, but we're talking about your future here, and your family or your future with your partner. Just keep running things over and over in your head – very, very important.

Keep storing the journey so far in your head. Big week coming up. You're near the finishing line.

WEEK SIX

FITNESS

DAY 1

Early morning: jogging 10 minutes, sprints four times one minute, 12 x burpees, 10 x 4 press-ups, 10 x 4 sit-ups, 5 x 6 squats, as many star jumps as you can in 10 minutes. Workout complete.

Early evening: 40-minute walk, 10 minutes basic stretching.

DAY 2

Early morning: mini workout, 10 x 3 press-ups, 10 x 3 leg raisers 10 x 3 sit-ups, 10 x 3 squats, 10 x 3 burpees. Finish off with 5 minutes running on the spot, 5 x one minute sets, 10 minutes basic stretching.

Mid-afternoon: 30 minutes swimming or a 30-minute bike ride.

Early evening: 20 minutes basic stretching.

DAY 3
Early morning: rest.

Mid-afternoon: 45-minute walk non-stop, when done do as many press-ups as you can. 5 minutes stretching.

Early evening: 20 minutes basic stretching.

DAY 4
Early morning: 10 press-ups, 10 sit-ups 10 leg raisers, 10 squats 3 x 1-minute plank exercise, finish with 10 minutes basic stretching.

Early evening: 10 minutes skipping, 10 mins bike ride and 10 mins dancing to music. Finish off with a 10-minute slow stretch.

DAY 5
Rest day.

DAY 6
Early morning: 30 mins jogging, 10 x 3 press-ups, 10 x 3 leg raises, 10 x 3 squats, 10 mins dance to music. Finish off with 10 mins stretching.

Mid-afternoon: 15-minute steady walk.

Early evening: 10 x 2 sit-ups, 10 x 2 press-ups, 10 mins sprinting, one min on and min off. Finish off with 40 squats, 10 x 4, and 10-minute stretch.

DAY 7
Rest day.

NUTRITION

DAY 1

Breakfast: small bowl of porridge oats with water or almond Alpro milk, add some blueberries and bananas. Slice of wholemeal toast with crunchy peanut butter. Decaf coffee or herbal tea. Always drink 3 litres of water per day.

Mid-morning snack: small protein shake, handful of almond nuts, one apple.

Lunch: green salad with ham off the bone, small portion of brown rice, one piece of brown pitta bread, no butter.

Mid-afternoon snack: 2 plain rice cakes or a protein bar or a glass of fresh fruit juice.

Evening meal: piece of white fish and a large portion of mixed veg, no rice or potatoes. Water, no coffee at all.

Late-night snack: Horlicks with water.

DAY 2

Breakfast: 3 fried eggs, one avocado, sliced, small portion of mushrooms, one tomato, grilled, no toast at all. Decaf coffee or herbal tea.

Mid-morning snack: an apple or a banana or a small handful of cashew nuts.

Lunch: one small sweet potato with sweetcorn, a small brown granary roll and no butter. Decaf coffee or herbal tea.

Mid-afternoon snack: no snack.

Evening meal: small seafood stir-fry, protein shake to follow.

Late-night snack: small Greek yogurt with honey.

DAY 3

Breakfast: one protein shake or home-made smoothie, one banana, black decaf coffee or herbal tea or fresh cranberry juice.

Mid-morning snack: 2 rice cakes with avocado spread on top, water or fresh fruit juice only.

Lunch: sliced large salad only, no dressing, one small pitta bread, no butter.

Mid-afternoon: no snack.

Evening meal: 1 x chicken breast, small portion of mixed veg and small portion of white rice. Small black decaff coffee or herbal tea.

Late-night snack: just a handful of dry roasted peanuts, Horlicks with water, go to bed.

DAY 4

Breakfast: 3 boiled eggs, no toast, a small sirloin steak, one protein shake, black decaf coffee, drink 3 litres of bottled water a day.

Mid-morning snack: Greek yogurt with honey, an apple or a banana.

Lunch: small portion of brown rice with a small salad, fresh cranberry juice.

No mid-afternoon snack.

Evening: 1 x tin of tuna in spring water with 2 sliced tomatoes, one brown roll, no butter.

Late-night snack: banana, Horlicks with water, go to bed.

DAY 5

Breakfast: granola with fresh fruit and Greek yogurt, one slice of wholemeal toast with 100% fruit jam, black coffee or herbal tea.

Mid-morning snack: a fruit flapjack.

Lunch: small jacket potato with baked beans, fresh cranberry juice.

Mid-afternoon snack: grapes or an apple with black decaf coffee.

Evening meal: A large takeaway of your choice, but don't go overboard.

Late-night snack: small chocolate bar of your choice.

DAY 6
Breakfast: Greek yogurt with honey, herbal tea.

Mid-morning snack: small protein shake or home-made smoothie.

Lunch: roast beef with mixed veg, no rice or potatoes.

No mid-afternoon snack.

No evening meal, just a large protein shake.

No late-night snack.

DAY 7
Breakfast: 2 poached eggs on 2 brown toasts, cooked tomatoes, fresh juice, small black decaf coffee.

Mid-morning snack: a banana with a small protein shake.

Lunch: prawn salad.

Mid-afternoon snack: a bag of mixed nuts or 2 rice cakes, crunchy peanut butter on top.

Evening meal: celebrate with a meal of your choice.

Late-night snack: celebrate with a small dessert of your choice.

MOTIVATION

DAY 1

Mindset and testWell, here we are – last week, and still going strong. Today, please think about all the terrible times you had when using cocaine, from the moment you wake up today until you go to bed tonight. For example: how you looked, how you felt, how you spoke, your feelings, your actions, your finances, your relationships. Today is about being as hard as you can on yourself – real deep thought.

Your mindset will focus on as many bad points as you can about your cocaine addiction and your journey, and the pain you caused yourself and family and loved ones whilst on the gear.

Keep thinking about all those nights when you were up in the early hours sniffing cocaine. With these memories, you must be hard on yourself all day.

You'll be feeling fed-up of running yourself down, looking forward to bed and sleep before you go to bed.

Look at those pieces of paper all around your house or flat, showing the amount of money you spent on cocaine.

DAY 2

MindsetDisconnect from any thoughts about cocaine. Take your mind elsewhere all day. Think about work issues, upgrading your training, or maybe think about how you can improve your and your family's way of life. Think about these plans all day.

Don't let any thought of cocaine issues come into your mind at all – very important. (Disconnect from any thoughts of cocaine, all day and all night).

Remember, no cocaine thoughts at all – very, very important.

DAY 3

MindsetYour cocaine habit is dying a slow death. Cocaine is no longer a substance you require or need to function on a daily basis. This was my mindset on the last week of my journey, and it needs to be yours.

I watched as many clips as possible on YouTube about cocaine addiction. I watched scared faces. Twice in the evening I made a point of looking at as many stories as I could about people who had been locked up over cocaine – drug dealers etc. All day, all night, I made it 24 hours entirely about all aspects of the drug, from films, YouTube, newspaper stories, and of course remembering the dramas it brought me. So today is 1000% about the drug, every minute of the day.

You'll be thinking cocaine, cocaine, cocaine, non-stop, so at the end of the day you'll be overcome by thinking about the drug. "This is crazy," you'll be thinking.

Your mindset will be cocaine, cocaine, cocaine, non-stop.Non-stop, thinking cocaine addiction, cocaine addiction, cocaine addiction, even late at night – plant that in your mind.

DAY 4

Mindset Just focus again on all the money you've spent and wasted on cocaine. Then look at the things you could have done. So today is about the amount of money you've spent on the drug. Run it over and over again in your mind, 24/7. Just plant that figure in your mind. You will be well pissed-off, trust me.

- Money wasted
- Money wasted
- Money wasted
- Wages gone

- Wages gone
- Wages gone

Late-night mindset: money wasted, money wasted, money wasted – even when you're in bed – think of money wasted on cocaine. You'll be well fed-up!

DAY 5

Mindset

Simple: just have a normal day like normal people, as in work, home, dinner, watch TV.

Back to basics, no thinking.

Normal day, no thinking.

Normal day, like normal people, no dramas at all.

Late-night mindset:

Simple living

Clean living

Clean mind

Go to bed with a simple mindset after a simple day.

DAY 6

Cocaine ruins lives. Look at the pieces of paper around your house / flat with the amount of money you've wasted on cocaine. Look at a picture of your mum and dad. Put in your old sim card and listen to all those stupid messages from your so-called coke-head friends. Keep looking back at yourself, remembering things like late nights, no money, feeling like shit. Cocaine ruins your life, cocaine ruins your mind.

Mindset Cocaine took control of your life.

Just do as I say please, people: I know it's a strange mindset but just sit tight, please.

DAY 7

Eyes open: you've made it! I just put you through a few days of hell. Everything you came across from thinking about your cocaine addiction journey, you have shut it down. The cravings don't exist any more. Even if they did, your powerful mindset would crush them severely.

Cocaine has lost the battle.

You, my friends, are at the finishing line. It's been tough. Take a moment to savour your happiness and victory. Everybody, male or female, is capable of disconnecting from the drug. Remember, you and only you made this happen. I gave you the ingredients, you have put them together. I salute you! Enjoy your new, clean life. WOW!!! What a feeling! You should be overcome with floods of tears, but tears of joy, not sadness.

Your 6-week plan is now finished.

Welcome to my world.